# The Evidences of the Christian Religion
## By Archibald Alexander, D. D.
### Edited by Anthony Uyl

Woodstock, Ontario, 2017

*The Evidences of the Christian Religion*
# The Evidences of the Christian Religion
By Archibald Alexander, D. D.
Edited by Anthony Uyl

--Ti de kai aph' heauton ou krinete to dikaion;
    Luke, XII. 57.

Originally Published by:
New-York: Jonathan Leavitt, Boston, Crocker & Brewster; 1832.

    Entered according to the act of Congress, in the year 1832, by WILLIAM D'HART, in the Clerk's office of the District of New-Jersey.

Originally Printed by:
D'Hart & Connolly, Printers, Princeton, N. J.

The text of The Evidences of the Christian Religion is all in the Public Domain. This edition is published by Devoted Publishing a division of 2165467 Ontario Inc.

**What kind of philosophies do you have?**
**Let us know!**

Contact us at: devotedpub@hotmail.com
Visit our shop on Facebook: @DevotedPublishing
**Published in Woodstock, Ontario, Canada 2017.**

For bulk educational rates, please contact us at the above email address.

ISBN: 978-1-77356-002-1

*Archibald Alexander, D. D.*

# Table of Contents

CHAPTER I - THE RIGHT USE OF REASON IN RELIGION..................................................4

CHAPTER II - IT IS IMPOSSIBLE TO BANISH ALL RELIGION FROM THE WORLD; AND IF IT WERE POSSIBLE, IT WOULD BE THE GREATEST CALAMITY WHICH COULD BEFAL THE HUMAN RACE..................................................8

    Footnote: ..................................................10

CHAPTER III - IF CHRISTIANITY BE REJECTED, THERE IS NO OTHER RELIGION WHICH CAN BE SUBSTITUTED IN ITS PLACE; AT LEAST NO OTHER WHICH WILL AT ALL ANSWER THE PURPOSE FOR WHICH RELIGION IS DESIRABLE..................................................11

    Footnotes: ..................................................15

CHAPTER IV - REVELATION NECESSARY TO TEACH US HOW TO WORSHIP GOD ACCEPTABLY--THE NATURE AND CERTAINTY OF A FUTURE STATE--AND ESPECIALLY, THE METHOD BY WHICH SINNERS MAY OBTAIN SALVATION..................................................16

CHAPTER V - THERE IS NOTHING IMPROBABLE OR UNREASONABLE IN THE IDEA OF A REVELATION FROM GOD; AND CONSEQUENTLY, NOTHING IMPROBABLE OR UNREASONABLE IN SUCH A MANIFEST DIVINE INTERPOSITION, AS MAY BE NECESSARY TO ESTABLISH A REVELATION ..................................................26

CHAPTER VI - MIRACLES ARE CAPABLE OF PROOF FROM TESTIMONY ..................................................28

    Footnotes: ..................................................32

CHAPTER VII - THE MIRACLES OF THE GOSPEL ARE CREDIBLE..................................................33

    Footnotes: ..................................................44

CHAPTER VIII - THE BIBLE CONTAINS PREDICTIONS OF EVENTS, WHICH NO HUMAN SAGACITY COULD HAVE FORESEEN, AND WHICH HAVE BEEN EXACTLY AND REMARKABLY ACCOMPLISHED ..................................................46

    Footnotes: ..................................................53

CHAPTER IX - NO OTHER RELIGION POSSESSES THE SAME KIND AND DEGREE OF EVIDENCE AS CHRISTIANITY: AND NO OTHER MIRACLES ARE AS WELL ATTESTED, AS THOSE RECORDED IN THE BIBLE ..................................................54

    Footnotes: ..................................................59

CHAPTER X - THE BIBLE CONTAINS INTERNAL EVIDENCE THAT ITS ORIGIN IS DIVINE.60

    Footnotes: ..................................................72

CHAPTER XI - THE SCRIPTURES OF THE OLD AND NEW TESTAMENT, WERE WRITTEN BY THE INSPIRATION OF GOD; AND THIS INSPIRATION, HOWEVER IT MAY BE DISTINGUISHED, WAS PLENARY; THAT IS, THE WRITERS WERE UNDER AN INFALLIBLE GUIDANCE, 130TH AS IT RELATES TO THE IDEAS AND WORDS: AND YET, THE ACQUIRED KNOWLEDGE, HABITS, AND PECULIAR DISPOSITIONS OF THE WRITERS, WERE NOT SUPERSEDED ..................................................73

NOTES..................................................82

    NOTE A - AN APPENDIX TO CHAPTER VI..................................................82

    NOTE B ..................................................86

    NOTE C ..................................................86

# CHAPTER I – THE RIGHT USE OF REASON IN RELIGION

THAT it is the right and the duty of all men to exercise their reason in inquiries concerning religion, is a truth so manifest, that it may be presumed there are none who will be disposed to call it in question.

Without reason there can be no religion; for in every step which we take, in examining the evidences of revelation, in interpreting its meaning, or in assenting to its doctrines, the exercise of this faculty is indispensable.

When the evidences of Christianity are exhibited, an appeal is made to the reason of men for its truth; but all evidence and all argument would be perfectly futile, if reason were not permitted to judge of their force. This noble faculty was certainly given to man to be a guide in religion, as well as in other things. He possesses no other means by which he can form a judgment on any subject, or assent to any truth; and it would be no more absurd to talk of seeing without eyes, than of knowing any thing without reason.

It is therefore a great mistake to suppose, that religion forbids or discourages the right use of reason. So far from this, she enjoins it as a duty of high moral obligation, and reproves those who neglect to judge for themselves what is right.

But it has frequently been said by the friends of revelation, that although reason is legitimately exercised in examining the evidences of revelation, and in determining the sense of the words by which it is conveyed; yet it is not within her province to sit in judgment on the doctrines contained in such a divine communication. This statement, though intended to guard against the abuse of reason, is not, in my opinion, altogether accurate. For it is manifest, that we can form no conception of a truth of any kind, without reason; and when we receive any thing as true, whatever may be the evidence on which it is founded, we must view the reception of it to be, reasonable. Truth and reason are so intimately connected that they can never, with propriety, be separated. Truth is the object, and reason the faculty by which it is apprehended; whatever be the nature of the truth or of the evidence by which it is established. No-doctrine can be a proper object of our faith which it is not more reasonable to receive, than to reject. If a book, claiming to be a divine revelation, is found to contain doctrines which can in no way be reconciled to right reason, it is a sure evidence that those claims have no solid foundation, and ought to be rejected. But that a revelation should contain doctrines of a mysterious and incomprehensible nature, and entirely different from all our previous conceptions, and, considered in themselves, improbable, is not repugnant to reason; on the contrary, judging from analogy, sound reason would lead us to expect such things in a revelation from God. Every thing which relates to this Infinite Being, must be to us, in some respects, incomprehensible. Every new truth must be different from all that is already known; and all the plans and works of God are very far above and beyond the conception of such minds as ours. Natural religion has as great mysteries as any in revelation: and the created universe, as it exists, is as different from any plan which men would have conceived, as any of the truths contained in a revelation can be. But it is reasonable to believe, what by our senses we perceive to exist; and it is reasonable to believe, whatever God declares to be true.

In receiving, therefore, the most mysterious doctrines of revelation, the ultimate appeal is to reason. Not to determine whether she could have discovered these truths; not to declare, whether considered in themselves, they appear probable; but to decide, whether it is not more reasonable to believe what God speaks, than to confide in our own crude and feeble conceptions. Just as if an unlearned man should hear an able astronomer declare, that the diurnal motion of the heavens is not real but only apparent, or that the sun is nearer to the earth in winter than in summer; although the facts asserted, appeared to contradict his senses, yet it would be reasonable to acquiesce in the declarations made to him by one who understood the subject, and in whose veracity he had confidence. If, then, we receive the witness of men, in matters above our comprehension, much more should we receive the witness of God, who knows all things, and cannot deceive his creatures, by false declarations.

There is no just cause for apprehending, that we shall be misled by the proper exercise of reason, on any subject, which may be proposed for our consideration. The only danger is, of making an improper use of this faculty, which is one of the most common faults to which our nature is liable Most men profess, that they are guided by reason in forming their opinions; but if this were really the case, the world would not be overrun with error; there would not be so many absurd and dangerous opinions propagated, and pertinaciously defended. They may be said, indeed, in one sense, to follow reason, for they are guided by a blinded, prejudiced, and perverted reason.

One large class of men are accustomed, from a slight and superficial view of the important subject of religion, to draw a hasty conclusion, which must prove, in the highest degree, detrimental to their happiness. They have observed, that in the modern, as well as ancient world, there is much superstition, much imposture, much diversity of opinion and variety of sects, many false pretences to Divine Inspiration, and many false reports of miracles, and prophetic oracles: and without giving themselves the trouble of searching diligently for the. truth, amidst the various contending claims, they draw a general conclusion, that all religions are alike: that the whole affair is a cheat, the invention of cunning men who imposed on the credulity of the unthinking multitude: and that the claims to Divine Revelation, do not even deserve a serious examination. Does right reason dictate such a conclusion as this? If it did, and we were to apply it to all other concerns, it would make a sad overturning in the business of the world. Truth, honesty; and honor might, on these principles, be discarded, as unmeaning names; for of all these there have been innumerable counterfeits, and concerning all of them, an endless diversity of opinion.

A second class, who profess to be men of reason, pay more attention to the subject of religion; but their reason is a prejudiced judge. They listen with eager-. ness to, all that can be said against revelation. They read with avidity the books written against Christianity, and but too faithfully treasure up every objection to religion; but her advocates. never obtain from them a fair hearing. They never inquire, whether the arguments. and objections which appear to them so strong, have not been refuted. With the means of conviction within their reach, they remain firmly fixed in their infidelity; and as long as they pursue this partial method of investigation, they must ever remain in the same darkness.

A third class, who wish to be considered as taking reason for their guide, are under the dominion of vicious passions; of ambition, avarice, lust, or revenge. Men of this character, however strong their intellect, or extensive their erudition, can never reason impartially on any subject which interferes with the gratification of their predominant desires; and as religion forbids, under severe penalties, all irregular passions and vicious indulgences, they pursue it with malignant hatred. As one well observes, "they are against religion, because religion is against them" Such men never reason calmly on the subject, and they are incapable of receiving any benefit from the arguments of others. They never think of religion but with a feeling of enmity, and they never speak of it but in the language of sneer, or abuse. There is no object which this race of infidels. have more at heart, than to root up every principle of religion from the minds of men, and to drive it from the earth, so that not one vestige of it might remain to give them torment. Voltaire may be considered as the leader. of this band; and his humble imitators, have been too numerous, in every Christian country.

But there is still another class of men, more distinguished, as masters of reason, than those who have been mentioned. They are the cold, speculative, subtle set of skeptics, who involve themselves. in a thick mist of metaphysics; attack first principles, and confound, their readers with paradoxes. The number of those who belong to this class, is, perhaps, not large, but they are formidable: for while the other enemies of the truth, scarcely make a show of reason, these philosophers are experienced in all the intricacies of a refined logic; so that in their hands, error is made to appear in the guise of truth. Should we yield ourselves to the sophistry of these men, they will persuade us to doubt, not only of the truth of revelation, but of our senses, and of our very existence. If it be inquired, how they contrive to spread such a colouring of skepticism over every subject; the answer is, by artfully assuming false principles as the premises of their reasoning; by reasoning sophistically on correct principles; by the dexterous use of ambiguous terms; by pushing their inquiries beyond the limits of human knowledge; and by calling in question the first principles of all knowledge. But it is not easy to conjecture what their motive is; most probably, however, it is vanity. They are ambitious of appearing more profound and acute than other men; and distinction is not so readily obtained in the common course, as by flying off in an eccentric orbit. It cannot be any sincere regard for truth, which influences them; for, upon their principles, truth and reason are equally worthless. They pull down every thing, but build up nothing in its place. Truth has no greater enemies in the world than this Pyrrhonic sect.; and it is to be lamented, that, sometimes, ingenious young men are caught in the wiles of their sophistry, and are led so far into the labyrinth of their errors, that they are never able to extricate themselves; and all their fair prospects of virtue and usefulness are obscured forever.

Before I leave the consideration of the various classes of persons, who, while they profess to be guided by reason, make an improper use of this faculty, I ought to mention a set of men, distinguished for their learning and ingenuity, who profess to receive the Christian revelation, and glory in the appellation of Rational Christians. They proceed on the plausible and (if rightly understood) correct principle, of receiving nothing as true, but what their reason approves; but these very men, with all their fair appearances of rationality, are chargeable with as gross a dereliction of reason, as can well be conceived; and, in regard to consistency, are more vulnerable, than any of those already mentioned. For, while they admit, that God has made a revelation, they insist upon the right of bringing the truths revealed, to the test of human judgment and opinion, and reject diem as unreasonable, if they do not accord with this standard. But. the declaration of God is the highest reason which we can have for believing any thing. To set up our opinion against the plain expression of his will, is surely presumption of the highest kind. Perhaps, however, I do not represent the case with perfect accuracy. Perhaps, no man is chargeable with such an inconsistency, as to admit a thing to be contained in an undoubted revelation, and yet reject it. The exact state of the matter is this. The Scriptures, it is admitted, contain a revelation from God; but there are many things in the Bible, which, if taken in the most obvious sense, are inconsistent with reason; now, as nothing inconsistent with reason can be from God, it is concluded, that this cannot be the true sense of Scripture. Accordingly, their wits are set to work, and their learning laid under contribution, to invent and defend some other sense. Upon these principles, a man may believe just as much, or as little as he pleases, of what the Bible contains; for it has been found that no text is so stubborn as not to yield to some of the modes of treatment which have been adopted:, But I maintain, that this whole procedure is contrary to, right reason. The plain course which reason directs us to pursue, is, after examining the evidences of revelation; and being satisfied, to come to the interpretation. of the Scriptures with an unbiassed mind; and in the exercise of a sound judgment, and with the aid of those helps and rules which reason and experience suggest, to obtain: the sense of the several parts of the document and although this sense may contradict our preconceived, opinions, or clash with our inclinations,. we ought implicitly to receive it; and not by a refined ingenuity, and labored critical process, extort a meaning, that will: suit our own notions. This is not to form our opinions by the Word of God, but to cut down the sublime and mysterious doctrines of revelation, to the measure of our. narrow conceptions. And thus, in the creed of many, called rational Christians, the divine system of heavenly truth is shorn of its glory, and comes forth little more than an improved theory of Natural Religion. There is no reason in this.

But what if the plain sense of Scripture be absolutely repugnant to the first principles of reason? Let that be demonstrated, and the effect will be, rather to overthrow the Scriptures, than to favor such a method of forming a theory from them. But no such thing can. be demonstrated. The reasonings by which it has been attempted to prove, that the doctrines, commonly called orthodox, are contrary to reason, are fallacious; and a similar mode of reasoning, on the truths of Natural Religion, will land us in atheism.

Deistical writers have been fond of representing faith, and reason as irreconcilable. They have insinuated, and even asserted, that revelation cannot be received without a renunciation of reason; and have affected to regret, that it should be subjected to the trial of a rational investigation, which they allege, it can by no means bear. This was a favorite topic with Morgan, Bolingbroke, Voltaire, and Hume. The last mentioned author, in the close of his far famed Essay on Miracles, uses the following language; "Our most holy religion is founded on Faith, not on reason, and tis a sure method of exposing it, to put it to a test, which it is, by no means fitted to endure."--And again: "Mere reason, is insufficient to convince us of its [the Christian Religion's] veracity, and whoever is moved by faith to assent to it, is conscious of a continual miracle, in his owns person, which subverts all the principles of his understanding."

On the insidious nature of this attack, I shall not stop to remark, except to observe, that it may be taken as a specimen, not only of Hume's method of treating Christianity, but of that of the whole tribe of deistical writers, until very recently, when they have come out boldly. Under the mask of friendship, and with the words of respectfulness on their lips, they have aimed the most deadly thrusts at the vitals of Christianity. But in regard to the sentiment; expressed in this extract, the friends of revelation utterly disclaim it, and hold it to be false and unfounded. The state of the controversy between Christians and deists, did not authorize any such assertion. The defenders of the truth have ever been ready to meet their antagonists on the ground of impartial reason. They have met them at every point, where they have chosen to make the assault; and I may safely say, that no deistical argument remains unrefuted, no infidel objection undetected and unexposed.. As. Mr. Hume wrote this immediately after finishing his argument against miracles, perhaps he felt a confidence, that he had achieved what none before were able to effect. But his confidence was premature: the argument which he claims the honor of having discovered, (though this might be disputed on good ground,) has been refuted, with a clearness of evidence, sufficient to bring conviction to any mind, but that of a sophist and a skeptic. But we shall have further occasion, in the sequel, to consider the force of Mr. Hume's reasonings against miracles.

It may, perhaps, require some apology, that a subject which has been so fully and ably discussed, in numerous volumes, should be attempted to be treated in a short essay. My only apology is, that the poison of infidelity is imbibed by many, who never have access to the antidote. It is much to be regretted that some of the books which are almost sure to fall into the hands of literary youth, are deeply tinctured with skepticism. How many read Hume and Gibbon, who never have seen the answers of Campbell and Watson. Now, if we can present, even a brief outline of the evidences of Christianity, to

*Archibald Alexander, D. D.*

those who may not be disposed to read larger works, we may be contributing, in some small degree, to prevent the progress of one of the greatest evils to which men are liable.

## CHAPTER II – IT IS IMPOSSIBLE TO BANISH ALL RELIGION FROM THE WORLD; AND IF IT WERE POSSIBLE, IT WOULD BE THE GREATEST CALAMITY WHICH COULD BEFAL THE HUMAN RACE

IT is not my object here, to consider religion as it is a matter of duty, or a means of obtaining happiness in a future world; for both these would be equally disregarded by those men who aim at the subversion of all religion. What I shall attempt, at present, is to state and establish the fact, that man is so constituted, that he must have some sort of religion.

And the truth of this will be manifest, from an inspection of the principles of human nature, and from the history of the world. Man has naturally a sense of moral obligation, a perception of the difference between right and wrong, feelings of remorse or approbation on the review of his conduct, fears of future retribution when he has committed a crime, and a propensity to pay religious homage to some object, visible or invisible. These are what have been called his religious feelings; and from them he has received the appellation of a religious animal. And certainly there is nothing by which man is so clearly distinguished from the creatures below him, as this capacity for religion; for whatever indications they give of sagacity in other matters, it is impossible to communicate to them any ideas of morality, or any impressions of a religious nature. Now, that these feelings are natural, and not adventitious, is manifest, because they are found to exist in men of all ages, of all countries, and in every different state of society. And hence, no nation, ancient or modern, has ever been found without some kind of religion. It would be as difficult to find a whole nation without religion, as to find one destitute of speech. Some travellers, it is true, from superficial observation, have reported that some savage tribes had no ideas of religion, and no species of worship; but on more accurate examination, it has been ascertained, that this was a mistake. And from our present knowledge of the nations of the earth, we are authorised to assert, that there is not one totally destitute of some sense of religion, and some form of worship. The same thing was well known to all the wisest men of antiquity. It is a fact from which both Plato and Cicero have derived many important conclusions. And these principles of our nature are so deeply radicated, that they never can be removed. Men may be induced to abandon their old religion, and to adopt a new one; but they never can remain long free from all religion. Take away one object of worship and they will soon attach themselves to another. If unhappily they lose the knowledge of the true God, they will set up gods of their own invention: or receive them from others. The history of all nations bears such ample testimony to this fact, that it cannot be denied. Now, this universality of religion evinces, in the clearest manner, that the principle is natural, that it is an essential thing in the constitution of man: just as the fact, that men are always found living in society, proves that the social principle exists, and is natural to man.

Atheistical men, have, indeed, attempted to trace all religious feelings, and all rites of worship, to the craft of priests, and policy of rulers; but this opinion is not only unsupported by historical testimony, but is most unreasonable in itself. For if there had not existed a predisposition to religion in the minds of men, such a design would never have been conceived; and if it had, all attempts to introduce into the minds of men, ideas so foreign to their nature, must have been abortive.

At any rate, such an imposition could not have tow tinned for so long a time, and could not have been extended to every tribe and nation in the world. If no sense of religion had existed in the minds of men, priests and politicians, however cunning, would have had no handle to take hold of, no foundation on which to build. Besides, it seems to be forgotten by the advocates of this hypothesis, that the existence of priests, supposes the previous existence of religion.

They have, moreover, alleged, that fear produced the gods. Be it so; it still confirms my position, that there is something in the nature of man which leads him to religion; and it is reasonable to conclude, that a cause which has operated uniformly, heretofore, will continue to produce the same effects as long as the world stands. It is impossible, therefore, to banish all religion from the world.

To what degree, atheists have succeeded, in divesting themselves of all religious impression, I do not pretend to know. That some men have gone to a great length in counteracting the constitutional tendencies, and extinguishing the feelings, of nature, is undoubtedly true; but there have been sufficient indications to lead to the opinion, that there is more of affectation than reality in the bravery of their profession. It is known that some of them have, above other men, been the slaves of superstitious fears; and that others, in times of extreme peril, as in a storm at sea, have, for the moment, renounced their atheism, and cried as earnestly for mercy, as those around them. Now, if these philosophers, with all their reasoning, are not able to erase all religious impressions from their own minds, it is vain to attempt to banish all religion from the world.

But suppose the great work achieved; and that every vestige of religion was obliterated; what would be the result? Would men remain without any objects of religious homage? Would they never again be afraid of invisible powers? Would the feelings of remorse at no time urge them to perform some sort of penance, or attempt some kind of expiation? Would no impostors and false prophets arise to deceive the world again with their dreams, fancies, and pretended revelations? They must have made but superficial observations on human nature, who think that none of these things would ever occur.

If those persons, therefore, who oppose Christianity, hope, by its subversion, to get rid of all religion, they do greatly deceive themselves. This work being accomplished, they would soon have more to perform in endless progression. Instead of the pure, mild, benignant, religion of Christ, they would soon find themselves surrounded by superstitions as foul and as false, as monstrous and as absurd, as any which the hot bed of paganism ever produced. Look into the heathen world, and see the abominations and miseries which inveterate superstition perpetuates in some of the fairest and most populous regions of the globe. Look at the savage tribes of Africa and America, and contemplate the cruel bondage of superstition, to which the people are subjected. Evils as great would soon grow up among us, were it not for the salutary influence of Christianity. Our forefathers, before they became Christians, were in the same degraded and wretched situation. And shall we curse our posterity by bringing back those evils from which our fathers escaped? It is a truth which should be proclaimed every where On the house tops, that it is the Bible, which has delivered us from the horrid dominion of superstition; and it is the Bible, which must prevent its return. Philosophy has had no hand in working out this deliverance from the horrors of idolatry. With all her celebrated schools and sages, she never turned one individual from the worship of idols; and she would be equally powerless in preventing the return of superstition, if other barriers were removed.

But, I proceed now to the second part of my proposition, which is, that if religion could be banished from the world, it would be the greatest calamity which could befal the human race.

It has formerly been a matter of discussion with the learned, whether the influence of superstition or atheism was most baneful on society. Plutarch, Bacon, Boyle, Warburton, and others, have handled this subject, in a learned and ingenious manner, and arrived at very different conclusions. However doubtful this question may have been considered in former times, I believe all reflecting men are now pretty well satisfied, that the question is put to rest forever. We have recently beheld the spectacle of a great nation casting off contemptuously the religion of their fathers, and plunging at once into the abyss of atheism. We have seen the experiment tried, to ascertain whether a populous nation could exist without the restraints of religion. Every circumstance was as favourable to the success of the experiment, as it could be. Learning was in its highest state of advancement; philosophy boasted of an approximation to perfection; and refinement and politeness had never been more complete among any people. But what was the result? It is written in characters of blood. It was as if a volcano had burst upon the, world, and disgorged its fiery flood over all Europe. Such a scene of cruelty, cold-blooded malignity, beastly impurity, heaven-daring impiety, and insatiable rapaciousness, the world never witnessed before, and, I trust in God, will never witness again. The only ray of hope which brightened the dismal, prospect was, that this horrible system contained in itself the principles of its own speedy downfall, Atheism has no bond of union for its professors; no basis of mutual confidence. It breeds suspicion, and consequently hatred, in every breast; and it is actuated by a selfishness which utterly disregards all the bonds of nature, of gratitude, and of friendship. To an atheist, fear becomes the ruling passion. Conscious of his own want. of virtue, of honor, and humanity, he naturally views his fellows in the same light, and is ready to put them out of the way as soon as they appear, in any degree, to become. obstacles to the accomplishment of his plans. Hence the bloody actors in this tragedy, after glutting their revenge, by shedding the blood of innocent Christians and unoffending priests, turned. their murderous weapons against each other. Not. satisfied with inflicting death on, the objects of their suspicion or envy, they actually feasted their eyes, daily, with the streams of blood which incessantly flowed from the guillotine. Never was the justice of heaven against impious and cruel men more signally displayed, than in making these miscreants the instruments of vengeance upon each other. The general state of morals, in France, during the period in which Christianity was proscribed, and atheism reigned, was such as almost exceeds belief. An eye-witness of the whole scene, and an actor in some parts of it, has drawn the following sketch:--"Multiplied cases of suicide; prisons crowded with innocent persons; permanent guillotines; perjuries of all classes; parental authority set at naught; debauchery encouraged by an allowance to those called unmarried mothers; nearly six thousand divorces within the single city

*The Evidences of the Christian Religion*

of Paris, within a little more than two years after the law authorized them;--in a word, whatever is most obscene in vice, and most dreadful in ferocity!" [1] If these be the genuine fruits of atheism, then let us rather have superstition in its most. appalling form. Between atheism and superstition, there is this great difference; the latter may authorize some crimes, the former opens the flood-gates to all. The one restrains partially, the other removes all restraint from vice. Every kind of religion presents some terrors to evil doers; atheism promises complete immunity, and stamps virtue itself with the character of folly.

But we must not suppose that the whole mass of the French people became atheists, during this period. Far from it. A large majority viewed the whole scene with horror and detestation; but the atheistical philosophers had got the power in their hands; and though a small minority of the nation, were able to effect so much mischief. But from this example we may conjecture, what would be the state of things, if the whole mass of people in a nation should become atheists, or be freed from all the restraints of conscience and religion. Such an event will never occur, but if it should, all must acknowledge, that no greater calamity could be imagined. It would be a lively picture of hell upon earth; for what is there in the idea of hell more horrible, than the absence of all restraint and all hope, and the uncontrolled dominion of the most malignat passions! But there would be one remarkable point of difference, for while atheists deny the God that made them, the inhabitants of hell believe and tremble.

## *Footnote:*

1. Gregoire.

*Archibald Alexander, D. D.*

# CHAPTER III – IF CHRISTIANITY BE REJECTED, THERE IS NO OTHER RELIGION WHICH CAN BE SUBSTITUTED IN ITS PLACE; AT LEAST NO OTHER WHICH WILL AT ALL ANSWER THE PURPOSE FOR WHICH RELIGION IS DESIRABLE.

IT has been proved in the former section, that it is necessary to have some religion. We are already in possession of Christianity, which, by the confession of deists themselves, answers many valuable purposes.--ht behoves us, therefore, to consider well, what we are likely to obtain by the exchange, if we should relinquish it. If any man can show us a better religion, and founded on better evidences, we ought, in that event, to give it up willingly; but if this cannot be done, then surely it is not reasonable to part with a certain good, without receiving an equivalent, in its place. This would be, as if some persons sailing on the ocean, in a vessel which carried them prosperously, should determine to abandon it, without knowing that there was any other to receive them, merely because some of the passengers, pretending to skill, suggested that it was leaky, and would sooner or later founder.

Let the enemies of Christianity tell us plainly what their aim is, and what they design to substitute in the place of the Bible. This, however, they are unable to perform and yet they would have us to consent to give up our dearest hopes without knowing what we are to receive, or whether we are to receive any thing, to compensate for the loss.

This is a point of vital importance, and demands our most serious attention. If it is really intended to substitute some other religion in the place of Christianity, we ought certainly, before we make the exchange, to have the opportunity of examining its claims, that we may know whether it will be likely to answer the purposes for which religion is wanted. To bring this subject fairly into view, let us take a survey of the world, and inquire, what it has to propose for our selection, if we should renounce Christianity.

There are only three things, in that event, between which we must choose. The first, to adopt some of the existing, or some of the exploded systems of Paganism; the second, to accept the Koran instead of the Bible; and the third, to embrace Natural Religion, or pure deism.

Few men have had the effrontery to propose a return to Paganism: yet even this has not been too extravagant for some whose names stand high as men of literature. The learned Gibbon has not, that I recollect, expressed his opinion, on this subject, explicitly; but it may be fairly inferred, from many things in his History of the Decline and Fall of the Roman Empire, that he deeply regretted the subversion of the old Pagan system, and that the progress of Christianity was far from affording him any pleasure.

But although he makes it sufficiently manifest, that, could his wishes have governed past events, the old system would never have been disturbed, and Christianity never have had a footing; yet we cannot say, whether he would have given his vote to have the temples rebuilt, and the Pagan rites restored. It is difficult to tell what he wished to accomplish, by his opposition to Christianity; or whether he had any definite view, other than to manifest his hatred to the Gospel and its Author.

Taylor, the learned translator of Plato, openly avowed his predilection for the religion of the Athenian philosopher, and his wish that it might be revived; and, speaks in contemptuous terms of Christianity, in comparison with Platonism; but he never could have supposed that to be a suitable religion for the bulk of men, which had not the least influence upon them, while the philosopher lived. This, then, would be no substitute for Christianity; for under its benign influence, even THE POOR HAVE THE GOSPEL PREACHED. UNTO THEM. But I have no doubt, that, if the truth could be ascertained, we should find, that this sublime genius derived some of his best ideas, directly or indirectly from the Scriptures; and that if he had lived under: the light of the Gospel, he never would

*The Evidences of the Christian Religion*
have spoken, of it as his translator has done.

In the time of the revolution in France, after some trial had been made of having no religion, D'Aubermenil proposed a new religion, in imitation of the ancient Persians. His plan was to have the Deity represented by a perpetual fire, and offerings made to him, of fruits, oil, and salt; and libations poured out to the four elements. It was prescribed, that worship should be, celebrated daily in the temple, that every ninth day should be a sabbath, and that on certain festivals, all ages should unite in dances. A few fanatics in Paris, and elsewhere, actually adopted the new religion, but they were unable to attract any notice, and in a hula. time sunk into merited oblivion.

It has been common enough to set up the Mohammedan religion, in a sort of rival comparison with Christianity, but I do not know that any have gone so far as to prefer the Koran to the Bible, except those few miserable apostates, who, after being long "tossed about with every wind of doctrine," at length threw themselves into the arms of the Arabian impostor. How far this religion will bear a comparison with Christianity, will be seen in the sequel.

Deism, or Natural Religion, is then, the only hope of the world, if the Christian religion be rejected. To this our attention shall now be turned. The first English deists extolled Natural Religion to the skies, as a system which contained all that man had need to know: and as being simple and intelligible to the meanest capacity. But strange to tell, scarcely any two of them are agreed, as to what Natural Religion is; and the same discordance has existed among their successors. They are not agreed in even those points, which are most essential in religion, and most necessary to be settled, before any religious worship can be instituted. They differ on such points as these; whether there is any intrinsic difference between right and wrong; whether God pays any regard to the affairs of man; whether the soul is immortal; whether prayer is proper and useful; and whether any external rites of worship are necessary.

But Natural Religion is essentially defective, as a religion for sinners, which all men feel themselves to be. It informs us of no atonement, and makes no provision for the pardon of sin. Indeed, if we impartially consider the law of nature, all hope of pardon must be relinquished, because it is a first principle of Natural Religion, that every one mill be rewarded or punished exactly according to his works: and therefore, if any man sin, he must suffer according to the demerit of his crime.

As this religion teaches no plan of atonement and forgiveness, so it inculcates no effectual method of reformation, or purification from the pollution of sin, and affords no aid to those who wish to live well, but leaves all to be performed by the mere strength of men, which, alas! is insufficient to bear up against the power of temptation. In those very points in which we want a clear response, Natural Religion is silent. It can do no more when its light is clearest, than to direct us in the way of duty, and to intimate the consequences of disobedience. Deists, then, must lead such lives of perfection, as to need no pardon, no regeneration, no aid, no reformation. The system is good for them, who can go through life without sin: it sets no hope before the mourning penitent.

Again, if deism be the true religion, why has piety never flourished among its professors? why have they not been the most zealous and consistent worshippers of God? Does not truth promote piety? and will it not ever be the case, that they who hold the truth will love God most ardently, and serve him most faithfully?--But what is the fact, in regard to this class of men? Have they ever been distinguished for their spirit of devotion? Have they produced numerous instances of exemplary piety? It is so much the reverse, that even asking such reasonable questions, has the appearance of ridicule. And when people hear the words "pious deist," they have the same sort of feeling, as when mention is made of an honest thief, or a sober drunkard.

There is no slander in making this statement for deists do not affect to be pious. They have no love for devotion. If the truth were known, this is the very thing they wish to get rid of; and if they believed, that professing themselves to be deists, laid them under greater obligations to be devout, they would not be so zealous for the system. Believe me, the contest is not between one religion and another, it is between religion and irreligion. It is impossible that a man a truly pious temper, should reject the Bible, even if he were unacquainted with its historical evidences. He would find it to be so congenial to his taste, and so salutry in its effects on his own spirit, that he would conclude that it must have derived its origin from heaven. But we find no such spirit in the writings of deists. There is not in them a tincture of piety; but they have more than a sprinkling of profane ridicule. When you turn to them from the Bible, you are sensible of as great a transition, as if you passed suddenly from a warm and genial climate into the frigid zone,. If deists expect ever to conciliate regard for their religion, they must appear to be truly pious men, sincerely engaged in the service of God; and this will have more effect than all their arguments. But whenever this event shall occur, they will be found no longer opposing the Bible, but will esteem it as the best of books, and will come to it for fuel, to feed the flame of pure devotion. An African prince, who was brought to England and resided there some time, being asked what he thought of the Bible, answered, that he believed it to be from God, for he found all the good people in favor of it, and all the bad people against it!

The want of a spirit of piety and devotion, must be reckoned the principal reason why the deists

*Archibald Alexander, D. D.*

have never been able to establish, and keep up, any religious worship among themselves. The thing has been attempted at several different times and in different countries; but never with any success.

It is said, that the first enterprise of this kind was that of David Williams, an Englishman, who had been a dissenting minister in Liverpool, but passing over first to Socinianism, and then to deism, went to London, where, being patronised by sonic persons of influence, he opened a house for deistical worship, and formed a liturgy, consisting principally of praise to the Creator. Here he preached for a short time, and collected some followers; but he complained that most of his congregation went on to atheism. After four years trial, the scheme came to nothing. There were neither funds nor congregation remaining, and the Priest of nature, (as Williams styled himself,) through discouragement and ill health, abandoned the project.

Some feeble attempts of the same kind have been made in the United States; but they are unworthy of being particularly noticed. [2]

Frederick II., the deistical king of Prussia, had once formed the plan of a Pantheon, in Berlin, for the worshippers of all sects and all religions; the chief object of which was the subversion of Christianity; but the scheme was never carried into execution.

The most interesting experiment of this kind, was that made by the Theophilanthropists in France, during the period of the revolution. After some trial had been made of atheism and irreligion, and when the want of public worship was felt by many reflecting persons, a society was formed for the worship of God, by the name just mentioned, upon the pure principles of Natural Religion. Among the patrons of this society, were men beloved for their philanthropy, and distinguished for their learning; and some high in power.

La Revelliere Lepaux, one of the directory of France, was a zealous patron of the new religion. By his influence, permission was obtained to make use of the churches for their worship. In the city of Paris alone, eighteen or twenty were assigned to them, among which was the famous church of Notre Dame.

Their creed was simple, consisting of two great articles, the existence of God, and the immortality of the soul. Their moral system also embraced two great principles, the love of God, and the love of man;--which were indicated by the name assumed by the society. Their worship consisted of prayers, and hymns of praise, which were comprehended in a manual, prepared for a directory in worship. Lectures were delivered by the members, which, however, underwent the inspection of the society, before they were, pronounced in public. To these were added some simple ceremonies, such as placing a basket of fruits and flowers on the altar. Music, vocal and instrumental, was used: for the latter, they availed themselves of the organs, in the churches. Great efforts were made to have this worship generally introduced, in all the principal towns in France; and the views of the society were even extended to foreign countries. Their manual was sent into all parts of the republic, by the minister of the interior, free of expense.

Never did a society enjoy greater advantages at its commencement. Christianity had been rejected with scorn: atheism had for a short time been tried, but was found to be intolerable: the government was favorable to the project; men of learning and influence patronised it, and churches ready built, were at the service of the new denomination. The system of Natural Religion, also, which was adopted, was the best that could have been selected, and considerable wisdom was discovered in the construction of their liturgy. But with all these circumstances in their favor, the society could not subsist. At first, indeed, while the scene was novel, large audiences attended, most of whom, however, were merely spectators; but in a short time, they dwindled away to such a degree, that instead of occupying twenty churches, they needed only four, in Paris; and in some of the provincial towns, where they commenced under the most favorable auspices, they soon came to nothing. Thus they went on declining, until, under the consular government, they were prohibited the use of the churches any longer; upon which they immediately expired without a struggle; and it is believed that not a vestige of the society now remains.

It will be instructive and interesting to inquire into the reasons of this want of success, in a society enjoying so many advantages. Undoubtedly, the chief reason was, the want of a truly devotional spirit. This was observed from the beginning of their meetings. There was nothing to interest the feelings of the heart. Their orators might be men of learning, and might produce good moral discourses, but they were not men of piety; and not always men of pure morals. [3] Their hymns were said to be well composed, and the music good; but the musicians were hired from the stage. There was also a strange defect of liberality in contributing to the funds of the society. They found it impossible to raise, in some of their societies, a sum which every Christian congregation, even the poorest, of any sect, would have collected in one day. It is a fact, that one of the societies petitioned government to grant them relief from a debt, which they had contracted, in providing the apparatus of their worship, not amounting to more than fifty dollars, stating that their annual income did not exceed twenty dollars. In the other towns, their musicians deserted them, because they were not paid, and frequently, no person could be found to deliver lectures.

Another difficulty arose--which might have been foreseen. Some of the societies declared themselves independent; and would not agree to be governed by the manual which had been received,

*The Evidences of the Christian Religion*

any further than they chose. They also remonstrated against the authority exercised by the lecturers in the affairs of the society, and declared, that there was danger of their forming another hierarchy. There were also complaints against them, addressed to the ministers, by the agents of government in the provinces, on account of the influence which they might acquire, in civil affairs.

The Theophilanthropists were, moreover, censured by those who had made greater advances in the modern philosophy, for their illiberality. it was complained, that there were many who could not receive their creed, and all such must necessarily be excluded from their society. This censure seems to have troubled them much; and in order to wipe off the stigma, they appointed a fete, which they called the Anniversary of the re-establishment of Natural Religion. To prove that their liberality had no bounds, they prepared five banners to be carried in procession. On the first was inscribed the word, Religion; on the second, Morality: and on the others, respectively, Jews; Catholics; Protestants. When the procession was over, the bearers of the several banners gave each other the kiss of peace; and that none might mistake the extent of their liberality, the banner inscribed, Morality, was borne by a professed atheist, universally known as such in Paris. They had also other festivals, peculiar to themselves; and four in honor of the following persons, Socrates, St. Vincent de Paule, J. J. Rousseau, and Washington;--a strange conjunction of names, truly! [4]

I have been thus particular in giving an account of this society, because the facts furnish the strongest confirmation of my argument, and are in themselves curious and instructive. After the failure of this enterprise, deists will scarcely attempt again to institute any form of public worship.

But among those philosophers who believe in the perfectibility of human nature, under the fostering influence of increasing knowledge and good government, there is a vague theory, of a kind of mental, philosophical religion, which needs the aid of no external forms. The primary articles of their creed is, that religion is a thing entirely between God and every man's conscience; that all our Creator requires, is, the homage of the heart; that, if we feel reverence, gratitude, and submission, towards him, and act our part well in society, we have fulfilled our duty;--that we cannot know how we may be disposed of hereafter, and ought not to be anxious about the matter. Whether this is expected to be the religion of philosophers only, or also of the unlearned, and the great mass of laboring people, I am unable to say. But I know, that such a system as this, will, to a large majority of every community, be equivalent to no religion at all. The great body of the people must have something tangible; something visible, in their religion. They need the aid of the senses, and of the social principle, to fix their attention, to create an interest, and to excite the feelings of devotion. But the truth is, that if the heart be affected with lively emotions of piety, it will be pleasant, it will be useful, and it will be natural, to give them expression. This will hold in regard to philosophers and men of learning, as well as others. Wherever a number of persons participate in the same feelings, there is a strong inclination to hold communion together; and if sentiments of genuine piety exist in the bosoms of many, they will delight, to celebrate, is unison, the praises of that Being, whom they love and adore. There is no reason why pious emotions, more than others, should be smothered, and the tendency to express them, counteracted. Such indeed will never be the fact. Out of the abundance of the heart the mouth will speak. Piety, it is true, consists essentially in the exercise of the heart; but that religion which is merely mental, is suspicious; at best, very feeble; is not likely to produce any permanent effect on the character or comfort of the person entertaining it; and cannot be useful to others in the way of example.

In the year 1802, when Christianity, which had been proscribed in France, was restored by an act of government, a speech was delivered by one of the councillors of state, which contains excellent sentiments, on the subjects here treated. One or two extract will not be unacceptable to the reader. "Science can never be partaken of, but by a small number, but by religion one may be instructed without being learned. The Natural Religion, to which one may rise by the effects of a cultivated reason, is merely abstract and intellectual, and unfit for any people. It is revealed religion which points out all the truths that are useful to men who have neither time nor means for laborious disquisitions. Who then would wish to dry up that sacred spring of knowledge, which diffuses good maxims, brings them before the eyes of every individual, and communicates to them that authoritative and popular dress, without which they would be unknown to the multitude, and almost to all men. For want of a religious education for the last ten years, our children are without any ideas of a divinity, without any notion of what is just and unjust; hence arise barbarous manners, hence a people become ferocious.--One cannot but sigh over the lot which threatens the present and future generations. Alas! what have we gained by deviating from the path pointed out to us by our ancestors? What have we gained by substituting vain and abstract doctrines for the creed which actuated the minds of Turenne, Fenelon, and Pascal?"

I think enough has now been said to establish, beyond all reasonable doubt, our second proposition, that if Christianity be rejected, there is no other religion which can be substituted in its place; or, at least, no other which can at all answer the purpose /or which religion is desirable.

It may also be observed, in conclusion, that the facts which have been adduced, not only serve to confirm this proposition, but furnish new and cogent arguments in proof of the proposition maintained in the preceding chapter.

## *Footnotes:*

2. The infidel meetings which at present (A. D. 1831) are held in some of our principal cities, and where male and female lectures are delivered, on Sunday, and at other times, are not intended to be, in any sense, worshipping assemblies; but their character is understood to be atheistical, and their object is to bring into ridicule and contempt, every species of religion, whether natural or revealed.

3. Thomas Paine was one of them.

4. Histoire de Theophilanthropie, par M. Gregoire.--See Quarterly Review for January, 1823.

## CHAPTER IV – REVELATION NECESSARY TO TEACH US HOW TO WORSHIP GOD ACCEPTABLY—THE NATURE AND CERTAINTY OF A FUTURE STATE—AND ESPECIALLY, THE METHOD BY WHICH SINNERS MAY OBTAIN SALVATION.

IT would be superfluous here to repeat what was said in the preceding chapter, respecting the need in which man stood of a revelation when he first proceeded from the hands of his Creator. The object which we have, at present, in view, is, to inquire, whether man, in the condition in which we now find him, and in which history informs us he has existed for ages, does not stand in urgent need of more light titan he possesses; and, whether, there are not some points of vital importance, concerning which he must remain in the dark, unless the knowledge of the truth is communicated to him by a revelation from God. Let it be understood, however, in what sense it is asserted, that a revelation is necessary. Of course, it is not meant, that there is any natural necessity for such an event; nor is it intended, that God is obliged by any necessity, to grant a revelation. The necessity contended for, relates altogether to the wants of man. It is found, that in all times, and littler all circumstances, he needs information, which he cannot obtain from the unassisted exercise of his own reason; or, at least, cannot obtain so satisfactorily from this source, as from divine revelation.

For even if it were possible, for a few philosophers of the highest order of intellect, by long and profound investigation, to discover all the truths absolutely necessary to be known; yet, for the bulk of mankind, it might be all important, to have these same things made known by divine revelation; because the great majority of our race have neither leisure nor ability for such tedious and difficult researches. But the truth, as made known by history, is, that on those very points, on which it is most needful that man should be instructed, the wise men of this world are as much at a loss as the vulgar. They reasoned much, and speculated as far as human intellect could go; but instead of clearly ascertained truth, they rested at last, in mere conjecture; or deviated into gross error.

Again, if the light of nature were sufficient to shed some light on the great truths needful to be known by man; yet a clear, well attested communication from heaven, might be of the greatest utility, by speaking decisively and authoritatively, in regard to matters, concerning which the conclusions of reason are feeble, and uncertain. To affect the conscience and influence the heart, it is highly important that religious truth should be attended with certainty, and should be felt to possess the sanction of divine authority. What men discover by the slow deductions of reason, is found to operate feebly on the conscience, compared with the persuasion, that God speaks to us, immediately, by divine revelation. In reasoning about the most important truths, men differ exceedingly from one another; and this very circumstance spreads doubt and uncertainty over all their speculations. When we peruse the discourses of the wisest of the heathen sages, and observe what darkness surrounded them, we cannot but feel commiseration for the imbecility of the human intellect; and, indeed, the best of them were deeply convinced of the insufficiency of their own reason, to guide them; and, sometimes, seemed to entertain a glimmering hope, that at some future period, and in some unknown way, divine instruction might be communicated to the erring children of men.

It is also more than probable, that the clearest and most important ideas which the heathen philosophers entertained, were not the discoveries of their own reason, or a light struck out from an observation of the works of nature, but rays of truth derived more remotely, or more directly, from divine revelation, as has been remarked in another part of this essay.

But, after all, it is an undeniable fact, that reason, aided as it was by tradition, left men to grope in the dark, and to fall into the most degrading idolatry. Indeed, although reason may teach that there is a God, and that he ought to be worshipped; yet, of what kind his worship should be in order to be acceptable, she never has made known, nor is it within the reach of her ability. All the rites of worship invented by man are altogether unworthy of God; and, truly, it is in the nature of things impossible, that men should devise a form of acceptable worship, for no service of this kind can be pleasing in the sight of God, which he has not himself appointed. Now, if men have lost the knowledge of the original institutions of religion; or, if these have become altogether corrupt, there must be a new revelation, before man will be able to render an acceptable service to his Creator. There is good reason to believe, t hat many of the. heathen rites of worship, are nothing else but corruptions of divine institutions, which were given to man by an early revelation. This seems especially to be the fact, in relation to sacrifices, which constituted an essential part of the worship of almost all ancient nations; and some vestiges of which have come down by tradition, among the most barbarous tribes. Reason, certainly, never taught men that shedding the blood and taking away the life of an animal, could be an acceptable sacrifice to the deity; or, that presenting it on an altar, and consuming it wholly or partially by fire, could be a propitiation for sin; and yet these mysterious ceremonies were almost as universal as the gift of speech. And between the sacrifices of nations, remote from each other, there has been remarked, a wonderful similarity in the circumstances of their sacred offerings; in the erection of altars; in the pouring out the blood: in dividing the animal into pieces; in combining the offering of salt, wine, bread, and incense, with the sacrifice of animals; in considering the blood and death of the victim, as expiatory for sin; in having an order of priesthood to officiate in these sacred rites, who were solemnly consecrated to the service, and considered more holy than other men; and when, only a small part of the animal sacrificed was consumed in the fire, in feasting on the remainder, within the precincts of the temple, or sacred enclosure. And this analogy may be traced even in the names, by which similar sacrifices were denominated among different nations. These, and many other striking resemblances, in the rites of ancient nations, go to prove, incontestably, that they must have had a common origin; and no account of this is half so probable, as that which ascribes sacrificial rites to an original revelation, which brings us to see the credibility of the Mosaic history, in regard to the origin of religious worship.

But supposing that any heathen nation should now be convinced of the absurdity of idolatry, and should become sensible of their obligation to render some kind of external homage to the great Creator, by what means could they learn what sort of service would be acceptable? Reason could not teach them what rites should be observed. Without a revelation from God, they must forever remain without. a form of worship; or, if they attempted to invent certain rites, all experience teaches, that these human inventions will ever be marked with human weakness; and reason herself intimates, that no worship, not appointed by God, can be acceptable to him. It appears then, that even if man were not a sinner, still he would need a divine revelation, to teach him how to render an acceptable worship to his Creator.

Some infidel writers have pretended, that it is a matter of indifference by what rites God is worshipped, and that he is equally pleased with the services of all nations, however different from each other in their mode of worship. This doctrine is utterly inconsistent with the dictates of sound reason. Upon this principle, even human sacrifices, which have been so common in the world, would be justified. And the most impure and abominable rites would be sanctioned by the Deity. The whole worship of Pagan nations, both in ancient and modern times, is detestable; and no one who has any just conceptions of the attributes of God, can persuade himself, that he ever could be pleased, with services so characterized by cruelty, impurity, and folly. Indeed, their worship is not directed to the true God, but to the false deities of their own invention. They sacrifice not to God, but to devils. They substituted for the. august Creator, creatures of almost every kind and species. No man, under the government of reason, can look into any heathen temple, without being shocked and cort founded with the degrading and abominable rites of idolatry. The more this subject is contemplated, the more clearly will the necessity of divine revelation be felt, and the greater will appear to be its value to the human race. Who can read an account of the mythology and idolatry of the ancient Egyptians, or of the modern Hindoos, and not be deeply impressed with the necessity of something, which might have the effect of dispelling this horrible darkness, and breaking asunder these cruel bonds of superstition?

Another argument for the necessity of a divine revelation, is, that without it man must remain ignorant of his origin, and his end; and utterly unable to account for the circumstances by which he is surrounded. He finds himself here upon the earth, and feels that he is borne along the stream of time with the rest of his generation, towards a dark gulph before him, which he perceives he can by no means escape. But when he inquires, respecting the origin of the human race;--when he seeks a solution of the enigma of his sinful, suffering, and mortal existence, he finds no one among the living or the dead, from whom he can obtain the least satisfactory information, on these points. All the traditions and histories of men are full of fables; and if they contain some rays of truth, they are so mingled with error, that no man can distinguish the one from the other. Leaving out of view the history contained in the Bible, and all that we can learn from others casts not a solitary ray of light on the points under consideration. We have no means of tracing up our race to its origin, and the deist can give no rational account of the wickedness of men, and of their sufferings and death. The darkness and uncertainty resting on these subjects, have led many, who rejected the authority of the Bible, to adopt most absurd and atheistical hypotheses, respecting the origin of man. Some have professed to believe, that the earth and its inhabitants have existed from all eternity--which is too absurd to require refutation. Others have amused themselves and their readers, with the idea, that originally, the human race was merely a species of monkey or baboon, and that by degrees they laid aside their brutal appearance and manners, and certain inhuman appendages, and having, in process of time, invented language, and the arts most necessary to provide for the clothing and shelter of the body, they gradually rose higher and higher in the scale of improvement, until they arrived at that pitch of refinement and civilization, which has been attained by the most polished nations. These, it is true, are rather atheistical than deistical hypotheses; but they serve to show how little light reason can shed on this subject; and, how much we need a divine revelation. For the deist can form no theory which can satisfy our reasonable desires. He can give no good reason for the moral condition and mortality of our race. He may say, that it is the law of our nature; but this is merely to declare the fact, and not to account for it.

But we might, perhaps, be contented to remain ignorant of our origin, if we could know what is to be our destiny, hereafter; and how far it is connected with our present character and conduct. Reason has exerted and exhausted all her resources, to demonstrate a future existence, and to place the immortality of the soul on an immovable basis. But what has been the result of all these reasonings? Why, a possibility, or, to say the most, a strong probability, that the soul survives the body. But this, of all others, is the point, on which we want certainty--absolute certainty. How painful to be involved in a cloud of doubt and suspense, when we look forward to futurity; and, especially, when descending into the grave, to have nothing to lay hold of, but the conclusions or conjectures of our own feeble reason? That I do not depreciate the force of the arguments for the soul's immortality, will appear, from the fact, that many of the heathen philosophers held, that the soul died with the body;--that of those who believed in a future existence, some were of opinion, that after the lapse of a thousand years, or some longer period, it would come to an end; others--and these very numerous--believed in the doctrine of metempsychosis, or the transmigration of souls from the body of one animal to that of another, in perpetual succession; and more still, had no other idea of immortality, than that the soul--which they thought was a particle of deity--would, at death, be refunded into the divine essence; which was virtually to deny its future existence, as to its distinct personality;--or, as possessing individuality, and consciousness. Even such men as Socrates, Plato, and Cicero, had no clear, consistent, and satisfactory views of this interesting subject: not because they neglected to exercise their cultivated and powerful intellect, upon it; for it was a subject, which more than all others engaged their thoughts;--but, because it was surrounded by a darkness which unassisted reason could not penetrate. O how glad would these sages have been to possess one ray of that revelation which our infidels foolishly despise! The earlier deists, generally admitted the doctrine of a future state of retribution, and affected to believe, that reason, was sufficient to establish the doctrine; but their successors, in modern times, or at least, a large majority of them, have either denied, or called into question, this fundamental doctrine. And if we should weigh impartially, all the arguments which have ever been adduced, in ancient or modern times, to establish this point, we would be obliged to confess that we needed further light. And from the very nature of the case, no one can give us an absolute assurance of our future and immortal existence, but God alone. It is an event which depends on his will, and nothing else. Arguments may be adduced, to prove that the soul is naturally immortal; but they prove no more than this, that the same causes which effect the dissolution of the body, can have no tendency to destroy the existence and activity of the soul. And what are called the moral arguments, only go to prove, that if God exercises a moral government over his creatures here, there must be a place for a just retribution hereafter. But we want, on this point, more certainty.--We want one to come from the other world, to tell us that there is a future state.--We want to hear the voice of God testifying, that there is not only a future state, but a day of righteous judgment. Here, every man can judge for himself, whether he needs a revelation.

This argument for the necessity of a divine revelation, will be corroborated by observing the state of religion and morals among all heathen nations. It has often been remarked, that the most certain method of ascertaining what reason is capable of accomplishing, is to see what she has actually done in time past; especially, when enjoying all the advantages of high culture and extensive information. In physical science, we may expect new discoveries by the exercise of reason: and the science of morals may in time come to be better understood; but if all nations, even the most civilized and learned, as well as the rude and barbarous, have utterly failed in forming correct opinions, on the most essential points of theology and ethics; and have, all of them, fallen into the most absurd and degrading errors; and have acquiesced in the most abominable and impure rites of idolatry; then, what can be more evident, than that they needed a divine revelation? Probably, one reason why the nations were left so long to walk in their own ways, was, to convince us of our own imbecility, and to prepare us to receive gratefully, when offered, this most comprehensive gift of God.

To do justice to this argument, would require volumes; but as the subject has been amply treated by Leland and others, 1 will pass it over, by remarking, that the abominable rites of Pagan worship, and the shocking cruelties and impurities which have ever been perpetrated under the sanction of every heathen religion, make but a faint impression on our minds, because we only hear the distant report of these things, and are often tempted to think, that the narrative of these horrible doings, must be too highly colored: but, the truth is, the half, and far more than the half, remains untold, and cannot be publicly told, without outrageously offending against decency. It is an awful thought, that for so long a time, so many millions of our fellow creatures have been under the cruel bondage of superstition;--a slavery which affects the mind, and is productive of more human misery than all other causes. And as, Paganism still exists, and as its evils are unmitigated by the lapse of time, it is an easy matter to compare the Christian with the heathen world.--Cast your eye over the map of the earth, and say, where is found the densest darkness? Where does the light of truth shine? Is not the line of demarkation between light and darkness visible? And is it not as evident, as any thing can be, that the Bible is a rich blessing to all who possess and read it? We might here, also, institute a comparison between those Christian nations which freely circulate the Scriptures, and those who lock them up in a dead language--but this we omit; and go on to remark, that he who is informed of the events which have occurred on missionary ground, in our own times, must have his eyes covered with thick scales of prejudice, if he does not acknowledge, that the Gospel is the richest benefit which can be conferred on Pagan nations. Either then, a vile imposture--a cunningly devised fable--has the power of reforming and civilizing the most degraded of the heathen tribes; or, Christianity is a Divine Revelation; and is still accompanied by the power of God, making it effectual to the illumination, conversion, and salvation of the gentiles. Let the deist take his choice between these two things. But here, permit me to ask, whether, if a company of deists had gone out to Africa, or to the Society or Sandwich islands, any such reformation would have been wrought? The reader will smile, at the idea of a deist turning missionary to the heathen; but this very feeling demonstrates, that deism is not to be the means of regenerating the world. If the deist was right, certainly he would be the only proper person to send on a mission, to convert the idolatrous world. But all are ready to pronounce the very idea to be ludicrous. What! a missionary society of deists!-- Why, they have no confidence in their own principles, in this respect; and no zeal for propagating them in such a field, and with such sacrifices, as the Christian willingly makes.

But why should I go to distant and heathen lands, to prove that a revelation is necessary, when we have proof enough before our eyes. In any of our populous cities, we may draw a visible line between that part of the population, who are under the light of evangelical truth, and those who place themselves out of the reach of all the direct rays of the Gospel. Between these two extremes, there is a large class, not properly reckoned with either; but let us, without caring for exact accuracy in our computation, suppose, that one-third of the adult population are regular church-going people, who hear the leading truths of the Gospel from Sabbath to Sabbath; and that another third seldom or never attend any place of public worship. Between these two classes of citizens, we can institute a comparison. Exceptions you may have to make on both sides, but taking them in mass, is there any room to doubt whether religion is useful and necessary? From which of these classes, permit me to ask, are our prisons crowded with inmates? Suppose, first, that all those who never read the Bible, and frequent no place of worship, were removed from among us, would the state of society be meliorated, or deteriorated? Or, again, suppose that all the church-going people should be translated to another country, what would then be the condition of society? If I am not egregiously erroneous in my calculations, on the former supposition, we should be able to dispense with most of our means of coercion and restraint, and would save the enormous expense of keeping up such an array of courts, police-officers, and prisons. And, on the latter supposition, all the wealth of the country would be insufficient to provide places of confinement, and means of support, for the guilty; or, to come nearer to the truth, our large towns would soon become as Sodom; or as a den of thieves: and, soon, the doom of Sodom would sink them, never to rise again.

But does any one think that this is not a fair statement of the matter, as it seems to take for granted, that there is no religion, nor can be any, without revelation?. I would request the person who makes this objection to tell me what kind of religion might be expected, if the Bible were banished from among us? Suppose then, instead of the hundreds of Gospel preachers, whose voices are lifted up on the first day of every week, to warn men of the danger of a sinful course, and to point out to them the way of life, all their pulpits should be filled with infidel lecturers, male and female; what, in your consciences, do you think would be the effect on morals and social happiness? We all know that many sinners have been converted by the faithful preaching of the Gospel; permit me to inquire, do you know, or have you heard of any transgressors being turned from the error of their ways, by attending on deistical lectures; or even on the theatre, that boasted school of morality? No doubt, some of my readers have heard of conversions at these places of fashionable resort, but not to righteousness--not to God, but the contrary. And, as I have happened to mention the theatre, I will further add, that I am far more afraid of the moral influence of this institution, than of that of deistical or atheistical lectures; not because it pleads for vice--this would not be tolerated--but because it draws thousands within the enchanted circle of temptation, and plunges thoughtless youth into the vortex of sensual pleasure, from which it is difficult to extricate them.

But I will admit, that there may be much religion, without revelation; the whole heathen world is a proof of it. Some men of the world, indeed, confound all religions, and all the ministers of religion together, as if they were all alike; whereas, true and false religion, are as dissimilar, as light and darkness; and I will repeat what I have already said in substance, and that is, that, the only effectual barrier to false religion, is to cultivate that which is true. Infidelity may serve to sweep away one form of superstition, but after awhile the tide will turn, and enthusiasm, or superstition, will come in like a flood; for, as we have shown, the people must have some sort of religion; and if you banish that which is true, rational, sober, and benevolent, you will soon be visited with the most absurd and degrading systems of wild fanaticism; and these will, when the fires of enthusiasm are extinguished, settle down, or rather grow up, into hideous forms of superstition. The Pagan religions had some mixture of truth derived from early tradition; for they were all, as we have seen, a corruption of the primitive worship of fallen man: but banish the Bible, and you will have in its place, either the dark horrors of atheism, accompanied with crime, in her polluted and blood-stained robe, or you will have the reign of superstition, chilling every generous emotion--degrading every noble affection--and blighting all domestic bliss.

Sometimes, a splendid temple rests upon a few solid pillars, and falls to ruin if they be removed. Thus, the peace and order, and comfort, of civil society, depend much on two institutions; for both of which we are indebted to revelation. The first of these, is, the SACRED INSTITUTION OF MARRIAGE: the second is, the RELIGIOUS OBLIGATION OF AN OATH, or solemn affirmation, which is virtually the same thing. Remove these, and the fair fabric of human happiness totters at once to its very base.

But the argument on which I chiefly mean to dwell, to evince the necessity of a revelation, is, that without it, we can never learn how sin can be forgiven, or the sinner saved. Admitting then, that reason can direct us with sufficient clearness, in regard to all our moral duties; and admitting, that if a man performs his duty, no more is required of him, and he may confide in the justice and goodness of God; and that, in pursuing this course, no evil will ensue, and the suitable reward will not be wanting.--I say, admitting all this, for argument's sake--yea more, that all men possess this knowledge: yet, I maintain, that in relation to the state in which man actually is, it amounts to nothing. It is one thing to have a system of religion which suits the case of an innocent being, and quite another to find out a plan by which A SINNER can obtain forgiveness. A citizen may know full well, that if he obeys the laws of his country, he will be protected by all upright magistrates; but if he has already violated the laws, and incurred a formidable penalty, the knowledge mentioned does not reach his case. What he needs now, is to know how he can obtain a pardon, and evade the vengeance of the violated law. In every such case, there is an absolute need of a declaration, or revelation, from the supreme power of the state, of a willingness to pardon, on some certain condition. In no government can a pardon be a matter of course, or provided for by the law itself: for, such a provision would be subversive of all government. It would be a complete nullification of the obligation and authority of the law. Here, then, the momentous question occurs, is man a sinner? Have all men transgressed the law of God? I am willing to waive the proof of this point, for the present, and to leave it to the decision of every man's conscience is there then a man, upon earth, who is not conscious of having violated the law of his nature, both by omissions of duty, and the actual commission of sin?

Assuming it then as a fact, that men are sinners, I ask, what does the light of nature teach, respecting the forgiveness of sin? I shall endeavor to demonstrate, that reason sheds not a ray of light on this fundamental point; and, therefore, that Natural Religion, if known ever so perfectly and universally, could not bring us the relief which we need. The main argument for the position which I have laid down, is short and simple. It is the dictate of right reason, that God is just, and will render to every one according to his character and conduct; and that his law, being wise and good, must not be violated with impunity. Can the deist conceive of an objection to this principle?--Certainly not. It must be considered a self-evident truth, with every theist who believes in the moral government of God. The case is plain, therefore, and as far as the dictates of reason extend, the sinner has no prospect before him but to suffer the just punishment of his offences, whatever that may be.

To suppose that reason can inform us that God will pardon our sins, is to suppose that its dictates are contradictory; for, to pardon, is the same as not to punish; but we have just seen, that the voice of reason is, that God is just, and will render to every man what he deserves. These two things are not compatible. Before I proceed further, I must put the reader on his guard, against loose and illogical reasoning, on a point so vital. I scarcely know a subject, on which most men appear to satisfy themselves with more vague and fallacious arguments. Some of the more common of these, it, will be my object now to consider.

In the first place, it is alleged, and with much confidence asserted, by many, that God is a Being of too much benevolence and kindness, to inflict severe punishments on his erring creatures. This suggestion--for it has not the shape of an argument--seems to give honor to God, while it is very soothing to the mind of the sinner. But when it is examined, it will be found to be rather an insult than an honor; for it supposes that the Ruler of the universe, out of kindness to a rebellious creature, will cease to be just:--that, rather than punish offences as they deserve, he will dishonor his own law. What sort of compliment would it be to an upright judge, among men, to say of him, that we were sure his

*Archibald Alexander, D. D.*

benevolence and compassion would prevent him from inflicting the penalties annexed to the laws? But, if the Judge of all the earth, does not act upon the principle of punishing all sin as it deserves, on what other principle does he act? Would any one say, by punishing it half as much as it deserves;--but this might be a severe suffering; therefore, the conclusion to which this reasoning must lead, is, that God's goodness will, altogether, and forever, prevent him from inflicting any punishment on sin, however atrocious it may be. Many, in our days, who are not called deists or atheists, but who are more dangerous, because they mingle some Gospel truth with their errors, greedily embrace, and zealously inculcate this very opinion. But look at its consequences. The infinitely perfect God will treat alike the most malignant rebel, and the most affectionate and obedient servant. He will, in his treatment of his creatures, manifest no more displeasure at sin, than be does towards the most perfect virtue. If such benevolence as this existed, it would be no moral perfection, but a defect. But no; God's attributes are never at variance. There is no goodness in God which forbids or prevents the fullest exercise of justice. If ever he chooses to rescue sinners from the consequences of their sins, it will not be by sacrificing his justice, but by fully satisfying it. But this is an affair of which mere reason knows nothing. But if the deist should insist, that all moral goodness consists in benevolence, and nothing else, and therefore God will not punish any one but for his own good, I answer, that the good of the whole is to be preferred, by a benevolent being, to the happiness of an offending individual; and in all communities, the general good requires, that transgressors should he intimidated and restrained by punishment; so that it must be proved, that the good of the universe does not require the punishment of the guilty, before any such conclusion can be drawn from the benevolence of God.

It is manifest, therefore, that the suggestion which we have been considering, however pleasing to the mind in love with sin, and however plausible at first sight, will not bear examination; and instead of tending to the honor of God, takes from him all that is estimable in moral character. It allows him no other excellence than an indiscriminate benevolence to his creatures, without the least regard to their moral character. Such a being would not be the object of veneration and esteem, by all holy intelligences. An infinitely good God may punish transgressors according to the demerit of their climes, without any disparagement of his goodness; and an infinitely just and holy God must punish sin. "Shall not the Judge of all the earth do right?"

Another suggestion, supposed by many to be a dictate of reason, is, that all the punishment ever inflicted on men for their sins, is the evil which arises out of it from the laws of nature, and the constitution of the human mind; and, that there is no good ground for any apprehension of any further or greater penalty. Now, let it be, in the first place, observed, that there is no proof adduced of the truth of this position; nor does it admit of proof. Who can tell what the Judge of all may think it necessary to inflict, hereafter, on sinners, for the manifestation of his justice, the vindication of his law, and as a terror to other offenders? Indeed, as far as we can judge of the facts, men do not suffer in this life, in any just proportion to their crimes: the wicked are often prosperous; and when the conscience becomes callous, they experience but little remorse for their worst crimes. Transgressors, who are only beginning their career, experience the agonies of an accusing conscience in the keenest manner; while the veteran in iniquity has long since ceased to be much troubled with these "compunctious visitations." But, supposing it true, that all the punishment of sin is that which naturally follows it, yet who can tell what all the consequences are, or where they will end? Crimes do not always produce their bitterest fruit, immediately. We see the sins of the intemperate, the lewd, and the dishonest, often overtaking them with their saddest consequences, long after the acts were committed. Sins committed in youth often produce a miserable old age. Look into the history of multitudes, whose vices have consigned them to a prison, or a mad house, and you will find that the cause of their wretchedness and disgrace, may be traced back to the sins of their youth: yes--those very sins, on which many are disposed to look with so indulgent an eye. And as these evils go on increasing until death, who can assure the sinner that this fearful progression will not continue beyond the grave? As we are not now arguing with atheists, we have a right to assume as a truth, the soul's future existence, and if it exist in conscious activity, will it not carry with it, the moral character acquired in this world? Will not the selfish, the proud, and malignant, be selfish, proud, and malignant, when the clay tabernacle is dropped? Can death transform a sordid, and guilty creature, into an angel? Will not the man who is wicked up to the moment of dissolution, continue to he wicked, after death? And will not he carry with him, his memory, his conscience, and his craving desires? There is then but little comfort for the sinner in this suggestion, if true; for he may find springing out of his own corruption, a worm which will never die,. and which will gnaw his vitals with as corroding a pain, as any which he is capable of enduring. Be it so, that conscience is the only fire to be dreaded in another world--who can tell us how intense and interminable the pain which this principle of our nature is capable of inflicting on the sinner? The fear, remorse, and horrible perturbation, which sometimes surround the death-beds of profligate sinners, afford a tremendous intimation, of what they may expect in a future, state. How great, or how long, the evil consequences. of sin may be, our reason certainly cannot tell; as far as her dictates extend, we can see no end to this progression in vice and misery.

*The Evidences of the Christian Religion*

But I come now to the consideration of a much more specious opinion, on which, deists, and others who agree with them in these matters, place great confidence. it is, that whatever the deserved penalty of sin may be, reason teaches us, that it can be set wide, or evaded, by a sincere and seasonable repentance. This principle has been assumed as a fundamental article in all the systems of sober deists. It is well known, that lord Herbert laid it down as one of the five positions, on which he founded his system; and, therefore, as perfectly understood by all men. And as many who wish to be considered rational Christians, adopt the same principle, it has gained very general possession of the public mind. And again, as pardon and repentance are closely connected, according to the doctrines of the Gospel, this truth of revelation, is by many, not distinguished from what is considered a dictate of reason; and hence it becomes a matter of real difficulty to separate truth from error, on this point; and in attempting it, we must encounter a formidable front of prejudice, not only from infidels, but also from others. And before I proceed further, I must request the reader to separate the evangelical doctrine of pardon, on repentance, from the deistical principle under consideration; for they stand on entirely different grounds, as will appear in the course of the discussion.

And here let it be carefully remarked, that before this doctrine of reason, as it is called, can become a practical principle, two things must be pre-supposed; first, that all men know what that repentance is, which will insure our pardon; and next, that every sinner has ability to perform it. The reasonableness of these pre-requisites is self-evident. But great difficulty attends the theory, as it relates to these points. For we would ask, whether by that repentance which reason inculcates, any thing more is meant than sorrow or compunction for our sins; or whether it includes a thorough reformation of life, and that not merely extending to external acts, but to the motives and affections of the heart? It is also reasonable to ask, whether any certain degree or continuance of sorrow is requisite? And whether repentance will not cease to be available, if the sinner revert to his former ways of iniquity? Moreover, whether repentance, flowing simply from fear of punishment, is genuine; and if not, what sort of principles must it have, as its source? It is also needful and important to inquire, whether an inveterate, hardened sinner, can repent of his sins, so as to hate and forsake them;--and surely no other repentance is worth any thing. With a mind filled with error, his conscience seared; and his habits deeply radicated, what hope is there of his turning about, and commencing a new life? From what principle could we anticipate such a change in a confirmed villain, or debauchee? You might as reasonably expect the Ethiopian to change his skin, as for him that has been long accustomed to do evil, to learn to do well. And it will answer no purpose to say, that he can repent if he will, and if he will not, the blame is all his own; for, we are inquiring, whether reason can teach a method of salvation adapted to the condition of sinners, and it matters not whether the obstacle be in the will or in something else: if it uniformly prevents the desired effect, it is plain, that something else is needed. And as to the blame being on his own head, it is admitted; but this is true in regard to every sin; for, in every act of transgression the sinner is culpable, otherwise it would be no sin; and if the only object be, to fix the blame upon the culprit, this is sufficiently provided for, without offering him pardon upon repentance; for, life and happiness can be secured, without repentance, if men will only obey the law of God perfectly. And there is no greater, nor other inability, in the way of his doing this, than in the way of his exercising true penitence. There is, manifestly, a radical defect in the deistical theory, on this very point; for it makes no provision for bringing the sinner to repentance, but merely offers pardon, in case he will do that to which his whole heart is averse. And does not fact accord with our sentiments? Where are the instances of deists repenting of their sins, and yet adhering to this system? There are indeed many glorious examples of infidels being brought to repentance and reformation, by the Gospel; but I would challenge the world to produce an instance of any one being brought to repentance, and a thorough change of life, merely on the principles of deism. And if the principle is in practice utterly ineffectual, of what value is it? and why should it be magnified into a matter of so much importance, as to be adduced as a proof that a revelation is not needed?

As, however, I wish to give a full and impartial discussion to this point, I will now, for the sake of argument, suppose, that the repentance which is necessary to pardon, is understood by all men, and that all have ability to perform it. The opinion then is, that all sinners by repentance may escape the punishment justly due to their sins; and this repentance they can bring into exercise, at any time, when it may be needed. Now, if this be true, and a dictate of reason, then it must be confessed, that a revelation is not absolutely necessary; for what method of salvation can be simpler, easier, or more intelligible than this? But, I deny that any such doctrine belongs to the system of natural religion, or is dictated by the light of reason. This opinion of the efficacy of repentance, is borrowed from the Gospel; and has been tacked to deism, with which: it has no coherence. The truth is, it is altogether incompatible with the first great fundamental principle of natural religion; namely, that God being just, will render to every one according to his moral character and conduct. And, here, I would repeat what has often been remarked by writers on this subject, that deists have ever been in the habit of borrowing from revelation, without giving' credit for what they take; and perhaps, without knowing whence the sentiment is derived. Men, born and educated under the light of revelation, however they may come to reject the

Bible, and all the positive institutions of Christianity, cannot divest themselves of all those important moral principles, which, directly or indirectly, they have derived from this source. The light of divine revelation is widely diffused in Christian countries, and has given complexion to all our laws, institutions, and systems of education; so, that a man can no more escape entirely from its influence, than, from the effect of the light of the sun. Many truths which the deist pretends to have discovered by the light of reason, are nothing else than the reflected light of divine revelation; for how else can you account for it, that the theory and moral system of our sober deists, should be so much superior to the attainments of Socrates, Plato, and Cicero? Their conduct resembles that of a man, who should light his taper by means of the sun's rays, and then pretend that all the light around him, he had struck out himself; or, that it was produced by the feeble taper which he held in his hand.

But, to return to the point under discussion. If a man, now he is a sinner, can certainly know that the punishment of his sins can be evaded by a repentance. completely in his own power, he could also know this before he sinned. Then, with the law written on his heart, and sanctioned with a penalty, he had the clear knowledge from reason, that commit whatever atrocious sins he might, and incur whatever punishment he might, that he would at any, and at every moment of his existence, have it in his power, to escape all the punishment which he had merited, simply by the act of repentance. This is a plain and fair statement of the case; and it is easy to see, that it is completely subversive of the law of God, as a binding rule; and leaves it fully in the power of the creature to do whatever he pleases. He may deliberately determine, that he will rebel against his Maker, till the last moment of life, and then disarm his vengeance, by repentance. The penalty of the law may be in itself, tremendous, but it can deter no one from any course which he may be inclined to pursue, because, he can, at any moment, remove himself from its operation. What greater license could the most daring rebel wish, than what is thus granted? This single principle admitted into the moral government of God, would be a complete nullification of the divine authority.

These consequences of the doctrine under consideration, are evident and inevitable, and demonstrate that it cannot be a principle of reason, or natural religion. But it may be thought by some, that the same objection will lie, with all its force, against the doctrine of the Gospel, which promises a plenary pardon to every true penitent. But this is a mistake: the evangelical doctrine of repentance stands on entirely different grounds. That such an offer would be made, could be known by no creature before he sinned. This doctrine does not in the least clash with the justice of God; for all the sins of the penitent, to which pardon is granted, are virtually and actually punished in the sinners substitute. Here is the grand point of difference between Christianity, and deism and all other systems. The former maintains the glory and harmony of all the divine attributes; the latter obscures, or would destroy one attribute, to make way for another. The consequence is, that the way in which pardon is granted to the penitent, according to the Gospel, has no tendency to relax our obligation to obedience, or to lessen our sense of the evil of sin; but the deistical principle of forgiveness, as we have seen, nullifies the law and authority of the Governor of the universe; and leaves it completely at the option of the creature, whether he will obey or transgress the law of God. The former is perfectly consistent with the justice of God, extending pardon to no sin for which satisfaction has not been made; while the latter is in direct repugnance to the clearest demands of justice.

But another objection to the opinion that the punishment of sin is remitted upon repentance, is, that this is contrary to experience, and fact. We have seen that the deist is fond of considering the punishment of win as being nothing else but its consequences, arising out of the laws of nature. Is it true, then, that the laws of nature change their course as soon as a sinner repents? Is it not a fact, that the penitent thief, in the penitentiary, and the repentant debauches, in the hospital, are still suffering the consequences of their crimes, long since committed? Repentance cannot bring back lost health, ruined reputation, dissipated fortune, and alienated friends. How then, can the deist, on his own principles, pretend, that the punishment of sin is removed by repentance? He may allege, that the future punishment of sin will be remitted; but how does he know this? reason can judge nothing in regard to the future, but by some analogy with what is observed to take place in this life; and from the facts stated, it is manifest, that all analogy is against the opinion, that the evil consequences of sin will be terminated by death.

Again, if pardon be granted only to the penitent; and the impenitent be punished according to the demerit of their crimes, then there is a state of sinning which renders it proper that sin should be punished rigidly according to its desert. There can, therefore, be no argument drawn from the goodness and compassion of God, against the condign punishment of sinners. But why is impenitence alone to be considered as exposing a sinner to the wrath of God? And why are the penitent alone, exempt from the penalty of the law? The answer must be, either, that the sin of impenitence is so great as to deserve this severe treatment; or, the merit of repentance is such as to atone for the greatest sins, which man can commit. But supposing that impenitence draws after it deeper guilt than all other sins, this does not prove that this alone should be punished; it only proves, that it should be punished more: but if there be a plain principle in jurisprudence, it is, that every sin should certainly be visited with punishment, but exactly according to its' nature. There is no reason why a less sin should be suffered to pass rather than a greater. Strict justice says, let every sin have its due retribution. The greatness of the sin of impenitence, therefore, cannot be a reason why the impenitent alone are to be punished. Nor can this great difference in the treatment of sinners, be owing to the merit of repentance; for it would be difficult to tell, wherein its most extraordinary merit consisted. It must either be in the obedience, or the suffering involved in the exercise of repentance. But it cannot consist in the degree of obedience which it contains; for, if this were perfect, it could do no more than answer the demands of the moral law, for the time being, but could have no effect on sins already committed. I think it a self-evident truth, that my obedience, this moment, cannot atone, or satify, for my disobedience, the preceding moment; for in the latter case, I do no more than my duty. Then, certainly, the obedience included in repentance cannot atone for all past sins, however enormous, for it is imperfect; and, moreover, has nothing in it which enhances its value, above other acts of obedience. Neither can the suffering involved in repentance atone for past sins; for, these pangs of compunction owe all their virtue to the obedience with which they are connected, and without which they would not even be of a moral nature. Unless some one should be of opinion, that these penitential sorrows are to be considered as an equivalent for the penalty of the law: but this cannot be correct, because an equivalent for the penalty of the law, would be an equal degree and duration of suffering. If, indeed, a person of higher dignity and greater worth is permitted to suffer in the place of another, in proportion to the difference in dignity, the sufferings may be diminished. It is, however, always a matter in the breast of the Supreme Judge, whether to allow of such a substitution. I see nothing unreasonable in it. But in the case under inquiry, the same person who owes the suffering, if I may so speak, endures the sorrows of repentance; and how, I would ask, can the pious grief of a few hours or days, be an equivalent for the punishment of the most heinous transgressions? Besides, the penitent sinner ever feels, and is ready to confess, that he deserves further punishment. No one who ever truly repented entertained the idea, that by this, he had made a complete atonement for his sins. These stains are of too deep a dye, to be washed out by a few penitential tears. Nothing can be more opposed to this opinion, than the views and feelings, involved in the exercises of true repentance. Every true penitent is deeply convinced, that he deserves heavier punishment, than what is involved in the sorrows which he now experiences.

There is, however, one ground for the opinion, that there is a reasonable connexion between repentance and forgiveness, which is, perhaps, more plausible than any other argument; and therefore merits a distinct consideration. It is, that all good men acknowledge, that it is a virtue to forgive those who offend us, when they appear to be penitent; and Christians cannot deny that this is a part of moral duty, for it is repeatedly and emphatically enjoined, in the New Testament, as a thing essential. What is here alleged, we fully admit; and are willing to go farther, and say, that it is made the duty of Christians to forgive those who injure them, whether they repent or not; for they are required to "love their enemies; to do good to them that hate them; to bless them that curse them; and pray for them which despitefully use them." But this is entirely a distinct case, and resting on principles entirely different, from the one under consideration. It is no part of the duty of Christians to inflict condign punishment on those who sin, even if they have been injured by them. They are forbidden to seek for revenge, or to render to the wicked according to their iniquities; not because there is any thing improper or inconsistent with moral goodness, in punishing the guilty as they deserve; but because this is the peculiar prerogative of the Governor of the universe. In those very passages of Scripture, where vengeance is forbidden to the creature, in express and emphatical language it is claimed for the Almighty. "Vengeance is mine, I will repay saith the Lord; therefore, if thine enemy hunger feed him, if he thirst give him drink, for in so doing thou shalt heap coals of fire on his head." If this duty of forgiveness, in the Christian, proved any thing, it would prove more than is wished; it would follow, that God would certainly pardon not only the penitent, but all sinners, however obstinate in their rebellion. But this conclusion is altogether at variance with the opinion which we have had under discussion, and is not even held up by the deist.

Another argument in favor of the doctrine that repentance is naturally connected with pardon, is derived from the practice of granting pardon, in human governments. But here, there is a mistake respecting the real state of the fact; for, although, it is true, that in all human governments, it is found expedient, to have a pardoning power, lodged somewhere; yet, no government ever yet professed to act on the principle of pardoning all offences, on the condition of repentance: nor, indeed, is the extension of mercy to certain criminals who have incurred the penalty of the law, at all connected with this principle. The reason why it is sometimes right to pardon offences against the state, is, either because in some particular case, the rigid execution of law would not be entirely just; or, that on account of the number of persons implicated, sound policy may dictate, that only the most guilty should be held up as an example. It appears, then, that the weakness of human governments is the ground on which the penalty of the law is remitted; but no such reason can exist in the divine government. But, in the execution of human laws, no inquiry is ever instituted, whether the criminal be penitent: yea, although his repentance should be most evident, yet this never disarms the law of its penalty. The penitent thief or murderer, are punished by our laws, as well as the obstinate and impenitent. If, in a few cases, rulers who possessed the power of granting pardon, have acted on the principle, that criminals who discovered signs of penitence, should be, on that account, pardoned, it only proves, that men entrusted with power may be misled; for undoubtedly, this principle carried out, would soon be subversive of all law. If the only end of punishment was the good of the culprit, then, indeed, such a course might be defended; but as long as the good of the community is the chief end of punishment, it never can be safe to offer pardon to all who profess repentance; or who, for a while, appear to be reformed.

I think it is manifest, from the preceding discussion, that the idea of a certain connexion between repentance and pardon, in the moral government of God, is not derived from the light of nature, but from the Gospel; and, therefore, if pardon is to be had in this way, it is only on the ground of the atonement of Christ; and not on account of any merit or efficacy in repentance, to take away the guilt of sin.

And if these views are correct, then is a divine revelation absolutely necessary to teach us, that God is willing to receive the penitent into favor; and to inform us, on what terms this is practicable.

## CHAPTER V – THERE IS NOTHING IMPROBABLE OR UNREASONABLE IN THE IDEA OF A REVELATION FROM GOD; AND CONSEQUENTLY, NOTHING IMPROBABLE OR UNREASONABLE IN SUCH A MANIFEST DIVINE INTERPOSITION, AS MAY BE NECESSARY TO ESTABLISH A REVELATION

THAT a revelation is possible, will not be called in question by any who believe in the existance of a God; nor can it be believed that there is any thing in the notion of a revelation, repugnant to the moral attributes of the Supreme Being. It cannot be inconsistent with the wisdom, goodness, or holiness of God, to increase the knowledge of his intelligent creatures. The whole end of a revelation is to make men wiser, better, and happier; and what can be conceived more accordant with our ideas of divine perfection, than this?

That man is capable of receiving benefit from a revelation, is a truth so evident, that it would be folly to spend time in demonstrating it; for whatever may be thought of the sufficiency of Natural Religion, if it was fully understood and improved; yet all must admit, that men, generally, have not been sufficiently enlightened on the subject of religion. The history of the world, in all ages, proves the deplorable ignorance of the greater part of the human race, even on those subjects, which the advocates of Natural Religion, confess to be most important and fundamental, as has been proved in the preceding chapter.

It cannot be thought an unreasonable supposition, that when God made the original progenitors of our race, he should furnish them with such knowledge as was absolutely necessary, not only for their comfort, but for their preservation. As they were without experience, and had none upon earth from whom they could derive instruction, is it unreasonable to suppose, that the beneficent Creator communicated to them such a stock of knowledge, as was requisite for the common purposes of life? The theory of those who suppose, that man was at first a dumb, irrational animal, very little different from those which now roam the forest;--and that from this state lie emerged by his own exertions;--that he invented articulate speech, and all the arts of life, without ever receiving any aid, or any revelation from his Creator, has already been sufficiently refuted.

If, then, man received, at first, such ideas as were necessary to his condition, this was a revelation; and if afterwards he should at any time need information, on any subject connected with his happiness, why might not the benevolent Creator, who does not abandon the work of his hands, again vouchsafe to make a communication to him? Such an exigency, deists themselves being judges, did arise. Men, almost universally, fell into the practice of idolatry, and lost the knowledge of the true God. They betook themselves to the worship of the luminaries of heaven, of dead men, of beasts, and inanimate things. They invented superstitious rites, not only irrational, but cruel and abominable. These were transmitted from generation to generation; and the children became still more involved in ignorance, than their parents. Now, that the righteous Governor of the universe may leave men to follow their own inventions, and suffer by their own folly, is certain; for he has done so. But is it not consistent with his wisdom and goodness to use extraordinary means to rescue them from a state so degraded and wretched? Would not every sober deist admit, that some means of bringing them back to just ideas of Natural Religion would be desirable? If then the apostacy of man from his Maker should render some farther revelation necessary, would it not be highly benevolent to communicate whatever knowledge his circumstances required? Why would it be thought unreasonable, that God should sometimes depart from his common mode of acting, to answer great and valuable ends? What is there in the established course of nature so sacred or so immutable, that it must never on any occasion or for any purpose be changed?

*Archibald Alexander, D. D.*

The only reason why the laws of nature are uniform, is, that this is for the benefit of man, but if his interest requires a departure from the regular course, what is there to render it unreasonable? The Author of the universe has never hound himself to pursue one undeviating course, in the government of the world. The time may come when he may think proper to change the whole system. As he gave it a beginning, he may also give it an end. General uniformity is expedient, that men may know what to expect, and may have encouragement to use means to obtain necessary ends; but occasional and unfrequent deviations from this uniformity have no tendency to prevent the benefit arising from it. This is so evident a truth that I am almost ashamed to dwell so long upon it; but by the sophistry of infidels a strange darkness has been thrown over the subject, so that it seems to be thought that there would be something immoral, or unwise and inconsistent, in contravening the laws of nature.

Let it be remembered that the object here is not to prove that there must be a revelation; it is only to show that there would be nothing unreasonable in the thing; and farther, that it would be a very desirable thing for man, and altogether consistent with the perfections of God, and the principles on which he governs the world.

If God should determine to reveal his will to man, how could this be most conveniently effected? We can conceive of two ways. The first, by inspiring all who needed knowledge with the ideas which he wished to communicate. The second, by inspiring a few persons, and directing them to make known to others the truths received. The first would seem to be the most effectual, but the last is mose analogous to his other dispensations. Reason might have been given in perfection at once, and not left to the uncertainty of education and human improvement; but such is not the fact. By slow degrees and much culture this faculty attains its maturity, and when neglected never acquires any high degree of strength. In regard to the best mode of making a revelation, however, we are totally incompetent to judge; but of one thing we may be certain, that if God should give a revelation to men, he would so attest it as to enable all sincere inquirers to know that it derives its origin from him; for otherwise it would be useless, as there would be no evidence of its truth. Supposing a revelation to be given, what would be a satisfactory attestation of its divine origin? It must be some sign or evidence not capable of being counterfeited; something by which God should in some way manifest himself. And how could this be effected, but by the exertion of his power or the manifestation of his infinite knowledge? That is, by miracles, or by prophecies, or by both. There is then just as much probability that miracles will exist, (for prophecy may be considered one kind of miracle) as that a revelation will he given. The conjunction of these two things is reasonable; if we find the one, we may be sure the other exists also.

It is admitted that a revelation from God would have internal evidence of its origin, but this does not strike the attention at once. It requires time before it can be perceived; but in the first establishment of a revelation, there is need of some evidence which is obvious to the senses and level to the capacities of all. Just such an evidence are miracles. Moreover, internal evidence requires, in order that it may be perceived and appreciated, a certain favourable state of the moral feeling, without which it is apt to be overlooked, and produces no conviction; whereas external evidence is not only level to every capacity, but adapted to bring home conviction to every description of men, to the bad as well as the good.

Miracles then furnish the best proof for the establishment of a revelation. They seem to be its proper seal. They are the manifest attestation of God. Nothing can be conceived which will more strikingly indicate his power and presence than a visible suspension of the laws of nature. He is invisible: he must make himself known by his works, and a miracle is such a work as no other can perform. When therefore a person professes to have received a revelation from God, and when we behold the effects of Almighty power accompanying his words, all are sure that God is with him, and that he is a teacher sent from God; for otherwise he could never perform such wonderful works; or rather, to speak more correctly, God would never exert his power to confirm the pretensions of an impostor or to attest doctrines which are not true.

## CHAPTER VI – MIRACLES ARE CAPABLE OF PROOF FROM TESTIMONY

I do not know that any one has denied that a miracle would be credible, if exhibited to our senses. A man might, indeed, be deceived by an illusion arising from some disorder in his senses; but if he was conscious of being in a sound state of body and mind, and should witness not only one, but a variety of miracles; not only a few times, but for years, in succession; and, if he should find, that all around him had the same perceptions of these facts as himself, I need not say, that it would be reasonable to credit his senses, for the constitution of his nature would leave him no choice: he would be under the necessity of believing, what he saw with his eyes, heard with ears, and handled with his hands. But are there facts which a man would credit on the evidence of his senses, which can, by no means, be rendered credible by the testimony of any number of witnesses? Then there might be facts, the knowledge of which could never be so communicated as to be worthy of credit. According to this hypothesis, the constitution of our nature would require us to withhold our assent from what was true, and from what others knew to be true. If a thousand persons of the strictest veracity should testify, that they had repeatedly witnessed a miracle, and if all circumstances should concur to corroborate their testimony, yet upon this principle it would be unreasonable to credit them; even if they should consent to die in confirmation of what they declared to be the fact. This is the ground taken by Mr. Hume, in his boasted argument against miracles. But, it appears to me, that every man, previously to examination, must be convinced that it is false; for it is contrary to common sense, and universal experience of the effect of testimony. The true principle on this subject, is, that any fact which would be believed on the evidence of the senses, may be reasonably believed on testimony. For there may be testimony of such a nature, as to produce conviction as strong as any other conceivable evidence; and such testimony in favor of a miracle, would establish it as firmly as if we had witnessed it ourselves. But, notwithstanding this is the conclusion of common sense and experience, the metaphysical argument of Mr. Hume has had the effect of perplexing and unsettling the minds of many: and as he boasts, that "it will be useful to overthrow-miracles as long as the world endures," it seems necessary to enter into an examination of his argument, that we may be able to expose its fallacy. This has already been done, in a convincing manner, by several men, [5] eminent for their learning and discrimination: and if their works were read by all who peruse Hume, I should think it unnecessary to add a single word on the subject. But it may not be without use, to present a refutation, in a condensed form, for the sake of those who will not take the trouble to go through a minute and extended demonstration.

The argument of Mr. Hume will be best exhibited in his own words. "A miracle," says he, "supported by any human testimony, is more properly a subject of derision, than of argument. No testimony for any kind of miracle can ever possibly amount to a probability."--"We establish it as a maxim, that no human testimony can have such force, as to prove a miracle, and make a just foundation for any system of religion."--"Our belief or assurance of any fact from the report of eye witnesses, is derived from no other principle, than experience; that is, our observation of the veracity of human testimony, and of the usual conformity of facts to the reports of witnesses. Now, if the fact attested partakes of the marvellous, if it is such as has seldom fallen under our own observation; here is a contest of two opposite experiences, of which the one destroys the other, as far as its force goes. Further, if the fact affirmed by the witness, instead of being only marvellous, is really miraculous; if, besides, the testimony considered apart, and in itself, amounts to an entire proof; in that case there is proof against proof; of which the strongest must prevail. A miracle is a violation of the laws of nature; and as a firm and unalterable experience has established these laws, the proof against a miracle from the very nature of the fact is as entire as any argument from experience can possibly be imagined. And if so, it is an undeniable consequence, that it cannot be surmounted by any proof whatever from testimony. A miracle, therefore, however attested, can never be rendered credible, even in the lowest degree."

Here we have the substance of Mr. Hume's argument, on which I propose to make some remarks, intended to show that its whole plausibility depends on the assumption of false principles and the artful use of equivocal terms.

1. Some prejudice is created in the mind of the Unsuspecting reader, by the definition of a miracle here given. It is called "a violation of the laws of nature," which carries with it an unfavorable idea, as

though some obligation was violated, and some injury was done. But the simple truth is, that the laws of nature are nothing else than the common operations of divine power, in the government of the world, which depend entirely, for their existence and continuance, on the divine will; and a miracle is nothing else, than the exertion of the same power in a way different from that which is common; or, it may be a mere suspension of that power, which is commonly observed to operate in the world.

2. Mr. Hume's argument will apply to the evidence of the senses as well as to that derived from testimony, and will prove (if it prove any thing) that it would be impossible to believe in a miracle, if we should witness it ever so often. "The very same principle of experience," says he, "which gives us a certain degree of assurance in the testimony of witnesses, gives us also, in this case, another degree of assurance against the fact which they endeavor to establish, from which contradiction there arises necessarily a counterpoise, and mutual destruction of belief and authority." The very same counterpoise and mutual destruction of belief, must also occur between the assurance derived from the senses, and that derived from experience. The reason why testimony cannot be believed in favor of a miracle, is not, according to Mr. Hume, because it has no force; for taken by itself, it may be sufficient to produce assurance; but let this assurance be as strong as it may, it cannot be stronger than that derived from universal experience. "In that case," says he--"there is proof against proof." Now, it is evident, that upon these principles, the same equilibrium from contradictory evidence, must take place, between experience and the senses. If one evidence be stronger than another, "the stronger must prevail, but with a diminution of force in proportion to that of its antagonist." But in the case of the senses, and a firm and unalterable experience, the evidence is perfect on both sides, so that the "counterpoise and mutual destruction of belief," must occur. According to this metaphysical balance of Mr. Hume, a miracle could not be believed if we witnessed it ever so often; for although there is a great weight of evidence on each side, yet as there is an equilibrium, neither can have any influence on our assent. Whether Mr. Hume would have objected to this conclusion, does not appear; but it is manifest, that it logically follows from his argument, as much as in the case to. which he has applied it. And here we see to what a pitch of skepticism his reasoning leads.

3. Mr. Hume makes an unnecessary distinction between that which is marvellous, and that which is miraculous; for although there is a real difference, yet as to his argument, there is none. The force of his reasoning does not relate to events as being miraculous, but as being opposite to universal experience. If the conclusion, therefore, be correct, it will equally prove, that no testimony is sufficient to establish a natural event, which has not before been experienced. If ever so many witnesses should aver, that they had seen meteoric stones fall from the clouds, or the galvanic fluid melt metals, yet if we have never experienced these things ourselves, we must not believe them.

4. The opposite or contrary experience of Mr. Hume, in regard to miracles, can mean nothing more, than that such things have not been experienced. There is no other opposite experience conceivable, in this case, unless a number of persons present, at the same time, should experience opposite impressions. The distinction which he artfully makes, in relation to "the king of Siam, who refused to believe the first reports concerning the effects of frost," between that which is contrary to experience, and not conformable to experience, is without foundation. For a fact cannot be contrary to experience in any other way, than by being not conformable to it. There neither is, nor can be, any experience against miracles, except this, that they have not occurred in our own experience or that of others. When the proposition of our author is expressed in language free from ambiguity, it will amount to this, that what has never been experienced, can never be believed on any testimony; than which nothing can easily be conceived more false. In what a situation must man have been, at the beginning of the world, if he had adopted the principles of this skeptic.

5. Mr. Hume uses the word experience in a twofold sense, changing from one to the other, as best suits his purpose. Sometimes it means, personal experience, and at other times, and more commonly, the experience of the whole world. Now, if it be taken to mean our own individual experience, the argument will be, that no fact which we ourselves have not witnessed, can be established by testimony; which, if correct, would cut off, at a stroke, the greater part of human knowledge. Much the most numerous class of facts are those which we receive upon the testimony of others, and many of these are entirely different from any thing that we have personally experienced. Many learned men never take the trouble to witness the most curious experiments in philosophy, and chemistry; yet they are as well satisfied of their truth, as if they had personal experience of it.

But although an argument founded on an opposition between testimony and experience, in order to be of any validity, must relate to personal experience; yet, Mr. Hume commonly uses the term to signify the experience of all men in all ages. This extensive meaning of the term must be the one which be affixes to it in most places of his essay; because, it is an experience by which we know that the laws of nature are uniform and unalterable; and he has given an example which clearly determines the sense of the word,. "That a dead man should come to life," says he, "has never been witnessed in any age or country." Now, according to this use of the word, what he calls an argument, is a mere assumption of the point in dispute; what logicians call, a petitio principii;--a begging of the question. For, what is the

## The Evidences of the Christian Religion

question in. debate? is it not whether miracles have ever been experienced? And how does Mr. Hume undertake to prove that they never did exist? By an argument intended to demonstrate that no testimony can establish them; the main principle of which argument is, that all experience is against them. if miracles have ever occurred, they are not contrary to universal experience; for whatever has been witnessed at any time, by any person, makes part of universal experience. What sort of reasoning is it, then, to form an argument against the truth of miracles, founded on the assumption, that they never existed? if it be true, as he says, "That it has never been witnessed, in any age or country, that a dead man should come to life," then, indeed, it is useless to adduce testimony to prove, that the dead have, on some occasions, been brought to life. If he had a right to take this for granted, where was the use of such a parade of reasoning on the subject of testimony? The very conclusion to which he wished to come, is here assumed, as the main principle in the argument. It is, however, as easy to deny as to affirm; and we do utterly deny the truth of this position; so, that after all, we are at issue, precisely on the point, where we commenced. Nothing is proved by the argument which promised so much, except the skill of the writer in sophistical reasoning.

6. Our author falls into another mistake in his reasoning. The object is to prove, that testimony in favor of miracles, can never produce conviction, because it is opposed by uniform and unalterable experience. But how do we know what this universal experience is? Is it not by testimony, except within the narrow circle of our own personal experience? Then it turns out, that the testimony in favor of miracles is neutralized or overbalanced, by other testimony. That is, to destroy the force of testimony, he assumes a principle founded on testimony. It is admitted, that when testimony is adduced to establish any facts, if other and stronger testimony can be brought against them, their credibility is destroyed. But. if I bring testimony for a fact, and some One alleges that he can show that this testimony is unworthy of credit, because he can bring witnesses to prove that many persons in different countries and ages never saw any such thing; to such a person I would reply, that even if these witnesses declared the truth, it could not overthrow the positive testimony which I had adduced, as they did not contradict the facts asserted; and, besides, it must be determined, which witnesses are the most credible, yours or mine. Just so it is in the case of Mr. Hume's argument. He sets up uniform experience against testimony, and gives a preponderance to the former, on the ground, that witnesses are known sometimes to lie; but all that he knows of what has happened in other ages-and countries, is by testimony; and they who give this testimony are as fallible as others; therefore, there existed no ground for preferring the evidence of experience, to testimony. Besides, he is not in possession of testimony to establish a thousandth part of what has been experienced; and as far as it goes, it amounts to no more than non-experience; a mere negative thing, which can never have any weight to overthrow the testimony of positive witnesses. In a court of justice, such a method of rebutting testimony, would be rejected as totally inadmissible. If we had sufficient evidence of a fact of any kind, that testimony would not be invalidated, if it could be proved, that no person in the world had ever witnessed the like before. This want of previous experience naturally creates a presumption against the fact, which requires some force of evidence to overcome: but in all cases, a sufficient number of witnesses, of undoubted intelligence and veracity, will be able to remove the presumption, and produce conviction.

7. Mr. Hume lays it down as a principle, that our belief in testimony arises from "experience; that is, observation of the veracity of human testimony." But this is not correct. Our belief in testimony is as natural and constitutional, as our belief in our senses. Children, at first, believe implicitly all that is told them: and it is from experience that they learn to distrust testimony. If our faith in testimony arose from experience, it would be impossible to acquire any knowledge from instruction. If children were to believe nothing that was told them, until they had made observations on the veracity of human testimony, nothing would ever be believed; for they would never arrive at the maturity and judgment necessary to make observations on a subject so complicated.

But although, I perceive, Mr. Hume's object in wishing to establish this false principle, was, to exalt the evidence of what he calls experience, above testimony; yet, I think, if we should concede it to him, it could answer him no purpose, since we have shown, that this experience itself, depends on testimony. Whatever use he can make, of this principle, therefore, against testimony, can be turned against himself, since his knowledge of what the experience of the world is, can only be obtained by the report of witnesses, who, in different ages, have observed the course of nature.

8. Mr. Hume, on reflection, seems to have been convinced, that his argument was unsound; for in a note, appended to his Essay on Miracles, he makes a concession, which entirely overthrows the whole. But mark the disingenuity, or shall I not rather call it, the malignity of the man, against religion, which is manifested in this only evidence of his candor. He concedes that there may be miracles of such a kind, as to admit of proof from human testimony, in direct contradiction to his reiterated maxim, and in complete repugnance to all his reasoning; but. he makes the concession with the express reservation, that it shall not be applied to the support of religion. He, however, not only makes this concession, but gives an example of such miracles, and of the testimony which he admits to be sufficient to establish it. "Suppose," says he, "all authors in all languages agree, that from the first of January, 1600, there was a

total darkness all over the earth for eight days; suppose that the tradition of this event is still strong and lively among the people; that all travellers bring us accounts of the same tradition, &c.--IT IS EVIDENT THAT OUR PHILOSOPHERS OUGHT TO RECEIVE IT FOR CERTAIN." And this is a part of the same Essay, in which it is said, "That a miracle, supported by any human testimony, is more properly a subject of derision than argument." "No kind of testimony for any kind of miracle can possibly amount to a probability, much less to a proof."

It might appear, that after so complete a renunciation of the principle which at first he so strenuously asserted, we might have spared ourselves the pains of a formal refutation. But not so. The author is resolved, that his concession shall be of no service, whatever, to religion. Hear his own words: "But should this miracle be ascribed to any new system of religion; men in all ages have been so imposed upon by ridiculous stories of that kind, that this very circumstance would be full proof of a cheat, and sufficient with all men of sense, not only to make them reject the fact, but even reject it, without further examination." I have heard of a maxim, which, I believe, the Jesuits introduced, that, that might be true in philosophy, which was false in theology; but I never could have expected that a philosopher, a logician, and a metaphysician too, would utter any thing so unreasonable, and so marked with prejudice, as the declaration just quoted. The fact was admitted to have such evidence, that. even philosophers ought to receive it as certain. But not if it is ascribed to a new religion. On this subject no evidence is sufficient. It is perfectly unexceptionable in philosophy; but in religion a sensible man will reject it, whatever it may be; even without further examination. The. circumstance of its being a miracle connected with religion, is sufficient, in his opinion, to prove it a cheat, however complete the testimony. The world, it seems, has been so imposed on by ridiculous stories of this kind, that we must not even listen to any testimony in favor of religious miracles. This author would, indeed, reduce the advocates of religion to an awkward dilemma. They are called upon to produce evidence for their religion, but if they adduce it, sensible men will not notice it; even if it is good every where else, it must go for nothing in religion. Upon these principles, we might indeed give up the contest; but we are not willing to admit that this is sound logic, or good sense. The reason assigned for proscribing, in this summary way, all the testimony in favor of religion, will apply to other subjects. Men have been imposed on by ridiculous stories in philosophy, as well as in religion; but when evidence is proposed, shall we not even examine it, because there have been impositions? This is the very reason why we should examine with care, that we may distinguish between the true and the false.

If it were true, that miracles had often been ascribed to new religions, it would not prove that there never were any true miracles, but rather the contrary; just as the abounding of counterfeit money is evidence that there is some genuine; for that which has no existence is not counterfeited. But the clamor that has been raised by infidels about new religions being commonly founded on miracles, or the pretence of miracles, has very little foundation in fact. Besides the Jewish and Christian religions, (which are indeed parts of the same,) it would, I believe, be difficult to designate any other, which claims such an origin.

After all that has been said of the false maxims of the Jesuits, I doubt whether any one could be selected so perfectly at war with reason, as this of the Scotch philosopher: nay, I think, I may challenge all the enemies of revelation, to cull from any Christian writer, a sentence, so surcharged with prejudice.

But, to do justice to Mr. Hume--although he seems to have closed the door against all discussion, on our part--yet, in one of his general maxims, he leaves us one alternative. The maxim is this, "That no testimony is sufficient to establish a miracle, unless it be of such a kind, that its falsehood would be more miraculous than the fact." An ingenious writer [6] has undertaken to meet Mr. Hume on his own ground; and has endeavored to prove, that the testimony of the apostles and early Christians, if the facts reported by them were true, is a greater miracle than any which they have recorded. But the maxim, as stated by Mr. Hume, is not correct. With the change of a single word, perhaps, it may be adopted, and will place the question on its proper ground. The change which I propose, is to substitute the word improbable, for miraculous. And it will then read, No testimony is sufficient to establish a miracle, unless the testimony be of such a kind, that its falsehood would be. more improbable, than the fact which it endeavors to establish. The ground of objection to the word miraculous, is, that it involves a false principle, which is, that facts are incredible in proportion as they are miraculous; which principle, he, in several places avows, and which is, indeed, a cardinal point in his system of evidence. But it is not true. There are many cases which might be proposed, in which, of two events, one of which must be true, that which is miraculous is more probable than the one which is merely natural. I will mention only one at present. Man was either immediately created by God, or he proceeded from some natural cause. Need I ask, which of these is most probable? and yet the first is miraculous; the second not. The plain truth is, that in all cases, the fact which has most evidence is most probable, whether it be miraculous or natural. And when all evidence, relating to a proposition, is before the mind, THAT IS TRUE, WHICH IS EASIEST TO BE BELIEVED; because it is easier to believe with evidence, than against it.

We are willing, therefore, that this maxim, as now stated, should be the ground of our decision, and we pledge ourselves to prove, that, the falsehood of the miracles of the Gospel, would be more

*The Evidences of the Christian Religion*

improbable, and consequently more incredible, than the truth of the facts recorded in them. But this discussion will be reserved for another place. To conclude; since, it has been shown, that there is no antecedent presumption against miracles from the nature of God, or from the laws by which he governs the universe;--since, a miraculous fact is not more difficult to be accomplished by omnipotence, than any other;--since, miracles are no further improbable, than as they are unusual;--since, they are the most suitable and decisive evidences which can be given of a revelation;--since, even by the concession of Mr. Hume himself, there may be sufficient testimony fully to establish them:--and, since, the many false pretences to miracles, and the general disposition to credit them, are rather proofs that they have existed, than the contrary; we may safely conclude, that Mr. Hume's argument, on this subject, is sophistical and delusive; and that it is so far from being true, as he alleges, that they are incredible, whatever may be their evidence, when brought to support religion, that this is, of all others, that department, in which they are most reasonable and credible.

## *Footnotes:*

5. Dr. Campbell, Prof. Vince, Mr. Adam, Dr. Douglas.
6. Dr. Gleig.

Archibald Alexander, D. D.

# CHAPTER VII – THE MIRACLES OF THE GOSPEL ARE CREDIBLE

HAVING shown, in the preceding chapter, that miracles may be so attested as to be credible, I come now to examine the evidence by which the miraculous facts recorded in the New Testament, may be established.

This is the main point in our inquiry; for, after all that has been said, it must be admitted, that unless the Christian religion is attended with sufficient evidence, we cannot believe in it, even if we would.

Before entering directly on this discussion, it may be useful to premise a few things respecting the nature and force of testimony, which, it is presumed, will be admitted by all who have attended to the subject.

This species of evidence admits of all conceivable degrees, from the weakest probability to the fullest assurance; for while, on this ground, we yield to some reports, the most hesitating assent, we are as certainly persuaded of others, as of those things which we perceive by our senses, or have demonstrated by mathematical reasoning.

The exact force of testimony cannot be calculated by rule, nor estimated by reason; but is known, only from experience. Many things are believed on testimony, with the most unwavering confidence, when we are utterly unable to explain the precise ground on which our conviction rests. The sources of our information have been so numerous, and the same facts presented to us in so many forms, that it is impossible to attribute to each its influence in gaining our assent. If we were asked, on what particular testimony we believe there is such a place as Rome, or why we believe that such a person as Buonaparte lately figured in Europe, we could only answer, in the general, that multiplied testimonies of these facts, had reached us, so that all possibility of doubting was excluded. The same assurance, and resting on the same grounds, is experienced in relation to facts, which occurred in ages (; long past. Who can bring himself to doubt, whether such persons as Julius Cæsar, Paul, Mohammed, Columbus, or Luther, ever existed?

When we have obtained evidence to a certain amount, nothing is gained by the admission of more. The mind becomes, as it were, saturated, and no increase of conviction is produced, by multiplying witnesses. One sound demonstration of a theorem in mathematics, is as good as a hundred. A few upright witnesses who agree, and are uncontradicted by other evidence, are as satisfactory as any conceivable number. On a trial for murder, if there were a thousand witnesses who could attest the fact, a judicious court would not deem it necessary to examine more than half a dozen, or at most, a dozen, if there were a perfect agreement in their testimony. Experience only can inform us, what degree of evidence will produce complete conviction; but we may judge from former experience, what will be the effect of the same evidence, in future: and from the effect on our own minds, what it will be on the minds of others.

Testimony, not of the strongest kind, may be so corroborated by circumstances, and especially by the existing consequences of the facts reported, that it may be rendered credible, and even irresistible. Should a historian of doubtful credit attest, that an eclipse of the sun occured, on a certain day, and was visible in a certain place; if we possessed no other evidence of the fact, it might be considered doubtful, whether the testimony was true or false; but if by astronomical calculation, it should be found, that there must have been an eclipse of the sun at the time, and visible at that, place, the veracity of the witness, in this case, would be confirmed, beyond all possibility of doubt. Or, should we find it recorded by an anonymous author, that an earthquake, at a certain time, had overthrown a certain city; without further evidence, we should yield but a feeble assent to the statement; but if, on personal observation, or by the report of respectable travellers, it was ascertained, that the ruins of an ancient city existed in that place, we should consider the truth of the history as sufficiently established.

The evidences of the Christian religion may be sufficient, and yet not so strong as inevitably to produce conviction. Our conduct in the pursuit and reception of truth, may be intended by our Creator, to be an important part of the probation to which we are subjected; and, therefore, the evidence of revelation is not so great as to be irresistible; but is of such a kind, that the sincere and diligent inquirer will be in no danger of fatal mistake; while men of pride and prejudice, who prefer darkness to light,

*The Evidences of the Christian Religion*
will be almost sure to err. [7]

It is natural for all men to speak the truth; falsehood requires an effort. Wicked men lie, only when they have some sinister end in view. Combinations to deceive, are never formed, but with a view to accomplish some object desirable to those concerned. No set of men will be at the trouble of forging and propagating a falsehood, which promises them no profit or gratification. Much less will they engage in such an enterpriser with the view of bringing evil on themselves; or, when they foresee, that it can be productive of nothing,. but pain and reproach.

Between truth and falsehood there is so great a difference, that it is extremely difficult for the latter, so. effectually to assume the garb, and exhibit the aspect of the former, as, upon a strict scrutiny, not to be detected. No imposture can stand the test of rigid inquiry; and when the inquisition is made, the truth seldom, remains doubtful: the fraud is pretty sure to become manifest. The style and manner of truth are entirely different from those of falsehood. The one pursues a direct course, is candid, unaffected, and honest; the other, evasive, cunning, tortuous, and inconsistent; and is often betrayed, by the efforts made to avoid detection.

When both sides of a question are pressed with difficulties, reason teaches us to choose that which is attended with the fewest. Objectors to Christianity often forget to notice the difficulties of their own hypothesis. Every question has two sides--if we, reject the affirmative, we, of necessity, receive the negative with the consequences with which it may be burdened. If we reject the evidence of Christianity, and deny that miracles ever existed, we are bound to account for the existence of the Christian church, and for the conduct of the first preachers and primitive believers, on other principles. And whoever seriously undertakes this, will impose on himself a difficult task. Gibbon, has put forth his strength, on this subject, with very small success. His account of the origin of Christianity is very unsatisfactory, and is totally defective in historical evidence. [8]

If the evidences, on both sides of an important question, appear to be pretty equally balanced, it is the dictate of wisdom to lean to the safe side. In this question, undoubtedly, the safe side is that of religion; fir, if we should be mistaken here, we shall suffer no loss, and obtain sonic good by our error; but a mistake on the other side, must prove fatal.

When a proposition has been established by proper and sufficient evidence, our faith ought not to be shaken by every objection, which we may not be able to solve. To admit this, would be to plunge into skepticism, on all subjects; for, what truth is there to which some objection may not be raised that no man can fully answer? Even the clearest truths in science are not exempt from objections of this sort. It must be so, as long as our minds are so limited, and the extent of human knowledge so narrow. That man judges incorrectly, who supposes, that when he has found out some objection to Christianity which cannot be satisfactorily answered, he has gained a victory. There are, indeed, objections, which relate to the essence of a proposition, which, if sustained, do overthrow the evidence; but there are other numerous objections which leave the substantial evidence undisturbed. Concerning them, I speak, when I say, that objections, though not capable of an answer, should not be permitted to unsettle our faith.

Let us now proceed to the examination of the testimony for the miracles recorded in the Gospel. In this. discussion we shall take. it for granted, that such a person as Jesus Christ lived in. Judea, about the time mentioned by the evangelists;--that he inculcated a pure and sublime morality; lived a virtuous and unblamable life; and was put to death by Pontius Pilate, at the, instigation of the Jewish rulers. Also,. that his, apostles went forth into various countries preaching to the people, and declaring that this crucified Jesus was, a person sent from God,. for the salvation of the world; and that many were induced to connect themselves with the Christian church. These facts not being of a miraculous nature, and it being necessary to suppose-some such events, deists have commonly been disposed, to admit them. But Volney, in his Ruins, and some others, have imagined, that such a person as Jesus Christ never existed;--that this is the name of one of the celestial luminaries;--and that the Gospel history is an allegory. Such visionary theories do not deserve a serious answer; they are subversive of all historical truth, and have not a shadow of evidence. They may be well left to sink by the weight of their own, extravagance. Mons. Volney, however, has received a learned answer from a gentleman, [9] who has met him, on his own ground; and being as much attached to astronomical allegories as the Frenchman, has vanquished him with his own weapons.

In the examination of written testimony, the first thing requisite, is to prove the authenticity of the documents, in which it is recorded. The evidence, on which we depend, for the truth of the miracles performed by Jesus Christ, and by his apostles, is contained in the New Testament. Here we have four distinct narratives of the life, miracles, death, resurrection, and ascension of Jesus of Nazareth; and also a history of the acts and sufferings of the apostles in preaching the Gospel, and laying the foundation of the first Christian churches, after the resurrection and ascension of their Master. We have, also, in this collection of writings, a number of epistles, addressed to. the church in general, to particular churches, and to individuals. These, with a book of prophecy, corn-. pose the volume, called the New Testament.

These books are certainly not of recent origin; for there are extant, copies of the New Testament, in the. original Greek, which are, at the least, twelve hundred, years old. And before the time when these manuscripts were penned, we have, in other books, numerous testimonies to the existence of die Christian. Scriptures. They are not only mentioned, but quoted, expounded, and harmonized so that if every copy of. the New Testament had been lost, a large portion of it might be recovered, by means of the numerous quotations in the early Christian writers. Besides, there, are extant, versions of the New Testament, into several languages, made at a very early period. By these means, we are able to trace these writings up to the time, in which the apostles lived.

There is also ample proof, not only from Christian, but heathen authors, that a society, calling themselves Christians, existed as early as the reign. of Nero, who was contemporary with the apostles. It is evident, from the necessity of the case, that some such accounts as those contained in the Gospels, must have been received as true, from the first existence of the Christian church. Unless it had been preached and believed that Christ was a divine Teacher, and performed extraordinary works in attestation of his mission, how is it possible that such a society could have been formed? To suppose such a thing, would be to conceive of a, superstructure, without a foundation. The resurrection of Christ from the dead, must have been an article of the faith of Christians, from their very origin; for it is the corner stone of the whole edifice. Take the belief of this away, and the Christian system has no existence. There are also some external institutions peculiar to Christianity, which we must suppose to be coeval with the formation of the society, for they are the badges of the Christian profession, and constitute a part of their worship. I refer to baptism, and the eucharist. To suppose, that, in some way, Christianity first existed, and afterwards received these articles of faith, and these institutions of worship, is too improbable to be admitted by any impartial man. It would be to suppose that a religious society existed without any. principles; or that they rejected their original principles, and adopted new ones; and that they who imposed these upon them, had the address to persuade them, that they had always belonged to their system;--than which is not easy to conceive any thing more improbable. Let us, for a moment, attempt to imagine, that previously to the publication of the Gospels, the Christian Church had among them no report of the miracles, and no account of the institutions, recorded in these books. When they opened them, they would read, that their society was founded on the belief of the resurrection of Jesus; and that baptism and the eucharist were instituted by him before he left the world, and had existed among them ever since. Nothing can be more evident, therefore, than that the substance of what is contained in the Gospels, was believed and practised by Christians, from the commencement of the society.

As these books have come down to us under the names of certain apostles and disciples of Jesus Christ, so they were ascribed to the same persons, from the earliest mention of them. It is, by the ancient Fathers, spoken of as a fact, universally believed among Christians, and contradicted by nobody. And we must not suppose, that in the first ages of Christianity, there was little care or discrimination exercised, in ascertaining the true authors and genuine character of the books in circulation. The very reverse is the fact, The most diligent inquiries were instituted into matters of this kind. Other books were published in the name of the apostles, professing to give an account of. Jesus Christ, which were not genuine. The distinction between the books of the New Testament, and all others, of every class, was as clearly marked, in the earliest ages, as it has ever been since. The writings of the apostles were held in great veneration; were received by the churches, all over the world, as the rule of their faith, and directory of their lives; and publicly read at their meetings for the instruction of the people., When any controversy arose, they were appealed to as an authoritative standard. As soon as published, they were so widely scattered, and so carefully guarded, that no persons had it in their power to make any alteration in them.

The style, or dialect; in which these books are written, furnishes an evidence of their authenticity, of peculiar kind. It does not, indeed, ascertain the persons of the writers, but proves, that they must have been exactly in the circumstances of those to whom these books have been uniformly ascribed. The words are Greek but the idiom is Hebrew, or rather Syro-Chaldaic, the vernacular tongue of Judea, in the time of Christ and his apostles. This is a peculiarity which none could counterfeit, and which demonstrates, that the New Testament was not composed by men of a different country and age, from those in which the apostles lived.

In the New Testament, there are numerous references to rivers, mountains, seas, cities, and countries, which none but a person well acquainted with the geography of Judea and. the neighboring countries, could have made, without falling into innumerable errors. There is, moreover, incidental mention, of persons and facts, known from other authorities to have existed, and frequent allusions to manners and customs, peculiar to the Jews.

From all these considerations, it ought to be admitted without dispute, that these are indeed the writings of the apostles, and of those particular persons to whom they are ascribed. It would not, however, destroy their credibility, even if other persons had written them,. since they were certainly composed iai that age, and were received by the whole body of Christians. But what imaginable reason is there for doubting of the genuineness of these books? What persons were so likely to write books to guide the faith of the church, as the apostles? If they did not write them, who would? And why would they give the credit of them to others? But their universal reception, without opposition or contradiction, should silence every cavil. The persons who lived at this time, knew the apostles, and were deeply interested in the subject, and these are the proper judges of this question. And they have decided it, unanimously, as it relates to the historical books of the New Testament. From them the testimony has come down, through all succeeding ages, without a chasm. Even heathen writers and heretics are witnesses, that the Gospels were written by the persons whose names they bear. [10]

In other cases, we usually possess no other evidence of the genuineness of the most valued writings of antiquity, except the opinion of contemporaries, handed down by uncontradicted tradition. How soon would Homer be deprived of his glory, if such evidence was insisted on as is required for the genuineness of the New Testament? Certainly, as it respects evidence of genuineness, no books of antiquity stand upon a level with the books of the New Testament. The works of the Greek and Latin historians and poets, have no such evidence of being the writings of the persons whose names they bear, as the writings of Matthew, Mark, Luke, and John. For we have the testimony, not merely of individuals, but of numerous societies, widely scattered over the world. We have internal evidence, of a kind, which cannot be counterfeited. We have, in short, every species of evidence, of which the case admits. It may, therefore, be considered, as an established fact, that the books of the New Testament are the genuine productions of the apostles; and consequently, contain their testimony to the miracles of Jesus Christ, and also to those miracles, which, in his name, they performed after his ascension.

It is also certain, that the books of the New Testament have not undergone any material change, since they were written; for there is a general agreement in all the copies, in all the versions, and in all the quotations. There are, it is true, small discrepancies, which have occurred, through the ignorance or carelessness of transcribers; but, not more than might naturally be expected. There is no ancient book which has come down to us so entire as the Scriptures, and which is accompanied by so many means of correcting an erroneous reading, where it has occurred. This representation may appear surprising to those, who have heard of the vast multitude of various readings, which learned critics have collected from a collation of the manuscripts; but it ought to be understood by all who have ever heard of these discrepancies, that not one in a thousand of them, is of the least consequence;--that a great majority of them are merely differences in orthography, in the collocation of words, or in the use of words perfectly synonymous, by which the sense is not in the least affected. A cursory reader would find as little difference in the various manuscripts of the New Testament, as in the different printed editions of the English version.

Having established the authenticity of the record which contains the testimony, we shall next proceed to consider its credibility.

The serious and candid attention of the reader, is requested to the following remarks:

I. Many of the facts related in the Gospels, are undoubtedly of a miraculous nature. It is declared that Jesus Christ, in several instances, raised the dead;--in one of which, the person had been dead four days, so that the body began to be offensive to the smell. In every case, this miracle was wrought instantly, and without any other means, than speaking a word. It is declared, that he healed multitudes of the most inveterate and incurable diseases;--that he gave sight to the blind, hearing to the deaf, speech to the dumb, and active limbs to the withered and the maimed: that he delivered those who were furious and unmanageable, by reason of the possession of demons; that, on different occasions, he fed thousands of people with a few loaves and fishes until they were satisfied; and that the fragments which were gathered up, were much greater in quantity than the original materials; that he walked upon the sea, and with a word allayed the raging storm, and produced a great calm. And, finally, it is repeatedly and solemnly declared, by all the witnesses, that Jesus Christ, after being crucified, and after having continued in the sepulchre three days, rose from the dead, and after showing himself, frequently, to his disciples, ascended to heaven, in their presence.

That all these were real miracles, none can for a moment doubt. It is true, we do not know all the powers of nature; but we do know, as certainly as we know any thing, that such works as these could not be performed, but by the immediate power of God. The same remark may be extended to the miracles wrought by the apostles, in the name of the Lord Jesus; and especially, to that stupendous miracle on the day of Pentecost, when the Holy Ghost descended on the apostles, in visible form, and conferred on them the gift of tongues, and other extraordinary endowments. All must admit, that if these events ever occurred, then there have existed undoubted miracles.

II. The miracles of Jesus were performed, for the most part, in an open and public manner, in the presence of multitudes of witnesses, under the inspection of learned and malignant enemies; in a great variety of circumstances, and for several years in succession. There was here no room for trick, sleight of hand, illusion of the senses, or any thing else, which could impose on the spectators. This circumstance is important, because it proves to a certainty, that the apostles themselves could not be deluded and deceived, in the testimony which they have given. To suppose that they could think that they saw such miracles every day, for years, and yet be deceived, would be nearly as extravagant a supposition, as that we were deceived in all that we ever experienced.

III. The character of the miracles recorded in the Gospels, ought to be carefully observed. They were all worthy of the majesty, justice, and benevolence of the Son of God. They are characterized by dignity, propriety, and kindness. Most of them, indeed, were acts of tender compassion to the afflicted. Although so many miracles were performed, in so great a variety of circumstances, yet there is nothing ludicrous, puerile, or vindictive, in any of them. Christ never exerted his power to gratify the curiosity of any, or to supply his own daily wants. Ile made no ostentatious display of his wonderful power, and never used it to acquire wealth and influence. While he fed hungry multitudes by a miracle, he submitted to hunger and want himself; while he could command all nature, he remained in poverty;--not having so much as a home of any kind, to which he could retire to find repose. Although he was rejected and ill-treated by the Jews, yet he never refused to relieve any who sincerely sought his aid. His life, in consequence of the multitudes who flocked to him, was fatiguing, and on many accounts unpleasant, but he never grew weary in doing good.

Let any man compare the narrative of the miracles of Christ, contained in the genuine Gospels, with those fictitious accounts, which may be found in the apochryphal and spurious Gospels, still extant, and he will be struck with the remarkable contrast between them. The same result will be the consequence of a comparison of the miracles of Christ, with those, ascribed by the followers of Mohammed, to the impostor; or those contained in the legends of the church of Rome. I know not how any impartial man can read attentively the account of the miracles recorded in the Gospels, and not be convinced, from the very nature and circumstances of the facts reported, that they were real.

IV. There are no signs of fraud or imposture to be discovered in the record itself. There is, on the contrary, every indication of truth, honesty, and good intention, in the writers. Although they differ from each other in style and manner, so much, that it is evident, that the same person did not compose the four Gospels; yet there is a character of style which belongs to the whole of them, and which is without a parallel among any writers but the penmen of the Sacred Scriptures. It is an apparent exemption from the passions and frailties of human nature. The most stupendous miracles, are related without one exclamation of wonder from the historian: and without the least appearance of a desire to excite the wonder of the reader.

The character of Christ is drawn in no other way, than by simply telling what he did and said. There is no portraying of character in the way of general description, or by using strong epithets to set him forth. There is, perhaps, no such thing, in the Gospels, as an expression of admiration of any discourse or action, by the evangelists. If they relate such things, they are the words of others, which they faithfully set down. When they describe the sufferings of Christ, they never fall, as men usually do, into pathetic declamation. They are never carried away from their simple course by the power of sympathy. The facts are related, as though the writer felt nothing, but the strong purpose of declaring the truth, without giving any color whatever to the facts. Neither do they indulge themselves in those vehement expressions of indignation against the enemies of Christ, which we should naturally have expected. They never give utterance to a harsh expression against any one. They relate the treachery of Judas with the same unaffected simplicity, as if they had no feelings relative to his base conduct.

But there is something which exhibits the true character of the writers, in a light still stronger. It is the manner in which they speak of themselves. Few men can write much concerning themselves, without betraying the strength of self-love. Weak men, when they get on this topic, are commonly disgusting: and even when persons seem willing to let the truth be known, there is usually an effort discoverable, to seek compensation, in something, for every sacrifice which they make of reputation. But we may challenge any one to designate any instance, in which the least indication of this moral weakness has been given by the evangelists? They speak of themselves, and their companions, with the same candor, which characterizes their narrative in regard to others. They describe, in the most artless manner, the lowness of their origin, the meanness of their occupation, the grossness of their ignorance, the inveteracy of their prejudices, their childish contentions for superiority, their cowardice in the hour of danger, and the fatal apostacy of one, and temporary delinquency of another of their number. If any person supposes that it is an easy thing to write as the evangelists have done, he must have attended very little to the subject. The fact is, it cannot be imitated now, when the model is fully before us. That these unlearned men should be able to write books at all, with propriety, is a wonderful thing. Few fishermen, or mechanics, confined all their lives to laborious occupations, and untutored in the art of composition, could produce, without committing great faults, a narrative of their own lives. But that men of such an education should possess such self-command and self-denial, as is manifest in these compositions, cannot be easily accounted for, on common principles.

That, however, which deserves our special attention, is the absence of all appearance of ill design. I should like to ask a candid infidel, to point out, in the Gospel, some fact, or speech, which in the remotest degree, tends to prove, that the writers had a bad end in view. I need not say, that he could find nothing of the kind. Then, upon his hypothesis, we have this extraordinary fact; that four books, written by impostors, who have imposed on the world a series of falsehoods, do, in no part of them, betray the least appearance of ill design, or sinister purpose. Certainly, no other books, written by deceivers,

*The Evidences of the Christian Religion*
possess the same characteristics.

We have some instances of men of learning and piety, manifesting uncommon candor, in the accounts which they have left of their own errors, prejudices, and faults; but in all of them you perceive the semblance, if not the reality of human frailty. These works, however, are very valuable. Some eminent infidels, also, have come forward before the world, with CONFESSIONS, and narratives of their lives, and even of their secret crimes.

None has made himself more conspicuous in this way, than J. J. Rosseau, who professes to exhibit to the world, a full confession of his faults, during a period of many years. And to do him justice, he has exposed to view moral turpitude enough, to make, if it were possible, a demon blush. But this infatuated man gloried in his shame: and declared it to be his purpose, when called before the tribunal of Heaven, to appear with his book in his hand, and present it to his Judge, as his confession and apology. Through the transparent covering of affectation, we may observe the most disgusting pride and arrogance. While common sense and decency are outraged, by a needless confession of deeds which ought not to be once named, he is so far from exhibiting any thing of the character of a true penitent, that he rather appears as the shameless apologist of vice. By his unreserved disclosures, he aspired to a new sort of reputation and glory. Perhaps, there is not, in any language, a composition mom strongly marked with pride and presumption. His confessions were manifestly made, in a confidence of the corruption of mankind, from whom he expected much applause for his candor, and small censure for his vices; but as he has appealed, also, to another tribunal, we may be permitted to doubt, whether he will there find as much applause, and as slight condemnation, as he affected to expect. Between such impious confessions as these, and the simple, humble, and sober statements of the evangelists, there can be no comparison.

There is only, one other thing, in the style of the apostles, which I wish to bring into view. In all the detailed narratives which they have given of Jesus Christ, no allusion is ever made to his personal appearance. We are as much unacquainted with his stature, his aspect, his complexion, and his gait and manner, as if the Gospels had never been written. There is profound wisdom in this silence: yet I doubt whether any writers, following merely the impulse of their own feelings, would have avoided every allusion to tilts subject.

V. There is no just ground of objection to the testimony, on account of the paucity of the witnesses. In regard to most facts handed down to us by authentic history, it is seldom, that we have more than two or three historians, testifying the same things; and in many cases, we receive the testimony of one as sufficient, if all the circumstances of the fact corroborate his narrative. But here, we have four distinct and independent witnesses, who were perfectly acquainted with the facts which they relate. Two of these, Matthew and John, were of the number of the twelve, who accompanied Jesus, wherever he went, and saw, from day to day, the works which he performed. Mark and Luke might also have been eye-witnesses. Many think that they were of the number of the seventy disciples, sent out by Christ to preach; but if they were not, they might have been his followers, and have been often present, in Jerusalem and other places, where he exhibited his miracles. It is not necessary, however, to resort to either of these suppositions. They were contemporaries, early disciples, constant companions of the apostles, and travelled much among the churches. Mark was, at first, the companion of Paul and Barnabas, and afterwards, attached himself to Peter, from whose preaching, according to the universal tradition of the early Fathers, he composed his Gospel. Luke was chosen by the churches in Asia to accompany Paul in his labors, and was almost constantly with him, until his first imprisonment at Rome; at which time, his history of the life and labors of that apostle terminates

Besides these four evangelists, who have professedly written an account of the miracles of Jesus Christ, we have the incidental testimony of those apostles, who wrote the epistles, especially of Paul. It is true, Paul was not one of the twelve apostles who accompanied Christ on earth; but lie became an apostle, under such circumstances, as rendered his testimony as strong, as that of any other witness. He informs us, that he was met by Jesus near to Damascus, when he was "breathing out threatning and slaughter" against the disciples of Christ: who appeared to him in the midst of a resplendent light, and spoke to him. From that moment he became his devoted follower, and the most laborious and successful preacher of the Gospel. He abandoned the most flattering worldly prospects, which any young man in the Jewish nation could have. He possessed genius, learning, an unblemished character for religion and morality; was in high favor with the chief men of his nation, and seems to have been more zealous than any other individual, to extirpate Christianity. How can it be accounted for, that he should suddenly become a Christian, unless he did indeed see the risen Jesus? Instead of bright worldly prospects, which he had before, he was now subjected to persecution and contempt, wherever he went. The catalogue of only a part of his sufferings, which he gives in one of his epistles, is enough to appal the stoutest heart; yet, he never repented of his becoming a Christian, but continued to devote all his energies to the promotion of the Gospel, as long as he lived. This change, in a person of Paul's character and prospects, will never be accounted for upon principles of imposture, or enthusiasm. [11] Here, then, we can produce what. deists often demand, the testimony of an enemy. Not of one who was unconvinced by the evidence of Christianity, which would be an inconsistent testimony, and liable to great objections; but of one whose mind had been long inflamed with zeal against Christianity; and yet, by the force of evidence, was converted to be a zealous disciple, and retained, all his life, a deep and unwavering conviction of the truth of the Gospel. [12] This man, although he has not written a Gospel, has given repeated testimonies to the truth of the leading facts, which are now in question. Especially, he is one of the best witnesses on the subject of the resurrection of Christ; for he not only saw and conversed with Jesus after his ascension, but has informed us of some circumstances, of great importance, not mentioned by any of the evangelists. He asserts that Christ was seen by five hundred persons at one time, most of whom were still living when he wrote. If there had been any falsehood in this declaration, how soon must it have been detected? His letters, no doubt, were immediately transcribed, and conveyed to every part of the church; and how easy would it have been to prove the falsehood of such a declaration, if it had not been a fact? But almost every page of Paul's writings recognises as true, the resurrection of Jesus Christ. his constantly assumed as a truth most assuredly believed by all Christians. It is the great motive of exertion and source of consolation, in all his epistles. And when he would convince certain heretics of the absurdity of denying the resurrection of the body, he reduces them to this conclusion, that "if the dead rise not, then is Christ not risen," which would be, at once, to subvert the Christian religion. His appeal to the common assured belief of Christians, is remarkably strong, and pertinent to our purpose; "If," says he, "Christ be not risen, then is our preaching vain, and your faith is also vain. Yea, and we are found false witnesses of God; because we have testified of God that he raised up Christ, whom he raised not up, if so be that the dead rise not." Would any man in his senses, have written thus, if the resurrection of Christ had not been a fundamental article of faith among Christians; or if he had not been fully persuaded of its truth? Had Paul been an impostor, would he have dared to appeal to five hundred persons, most of whom were living, for the truth of what he knew to be false? How easy, and how certain, must have been the detection of an imposture thus conducted?

The same is evident from the epistles of the other apostles, and from the Apocalypse.

Now, when we can clearly ascertain what any persons believed in relation to a we have, virtually their testimony to that fact; because, when they come forward and give testimony, explicitly, they do no more than express the conviction of their own minds. Certainly, then, if we can by any means, ascertain what the primitive Christians believed in regard to the resurrection of Christ, and other miraculous facts, we are in possession of all the testimony which they could give. [13] This is an important point as it relates to the number of witnesses. Now, that all Christians, from the beginning, did believe in the facts recorded in the Gospels and Epistles of the apostles, we have the strongest possible evidence. It is proved incontestably, from the fact of their becoming Christians; for how could they be Christians without faith in Christianity? unless any one will be so extravagant as to believe, that not only the apostles, but all their converts, were wilful deceivers. It is proved also from the manner in which Christians are addressed by the apostles, in all the epistle. Suppose, for a moment, that the Corinthian church had no belief in the resurrection of Christ, when they received the above-mentioned epistle from Paul; would they not have considered him perfectly insane? But the universal reception of the Gospels and Epistles, by all Christian churches, throughout the world, is the best possible evidence that they believed what they contained. These books were adopted as the creed and guide of all Christians. It is manifest, therefore, that we are in possession of the testimony of the whole primitive church, to the truth of the miracles recorded in the Gospels. Suppose a document had come down to us, containing a profession of the belief of every person who embraced the Christian religion, and a solemn attestation to the facts on which Christianity is founded, would any man object, that the witnesses were too few? The fact is, that we have substantially, this whole body of testimony. I do not perceive, that its force would have been sensibly greater had it been transmitted to us with all the formalities just mentioned. There is, therefore, no defect in the number of witnesses. If every one of the twelve apostles had written a Gospel, and a hundred other persons had done the same, the evidence would not be essentially improved. We should have no more, after all, than the testimony of the whole primitive church, which, as has been proved, we possess already.

VI. The credibility of the testimony is not impaired by any want of agreement among the witnesses. In their attestation to the leading facts, and to the doctrines and character of Christ, they are perfectly harmonious. The selection of facts by the several evangelists is different, and the same fact is sometimes related more circumstantially by one, than another; yet there is no inconsistency between them. In their general character, and prominent features, there is a beautiful harmony in the Gospels. There is no difference which can affect, in the judgment of the impartial, the credibility of the testimony, which they contain. If all the evangelists had recorded precisely the same facts, and all the circumstances, in the same order, the Gospels would have the appearance of having been written in concert, which would weaken their testimony. But it is almost demonstrable, from internal evidence, that the evangelists, with the exception of John, never had seen each other's productions, before they wrote. Their agreement, therefore, ought to have the effect of witnesses examined apart from each other; and their discrepancies serve to prove, that there could be no concerted scheme to deceive; for in that case every appearance of this kind would have been carefully removed.

*The Evidences of the Christian Religion*

I am aware, however, that on the ground of supposed contradictions, or irreconcilable discrepancies, the most formidable attacks have been made on Christianity. It is entirely incompatible with the narrow limits of this essay, to enter into a consideration of the various methods which have been adapted for harmonizing the Gospels, and removing the difficulties which arise from their variations. I can only make a few general observations, with the view of leading the reader to the proper principles of solution.

It ought to be kept in mind, that the Gospels were written almost two thousand years ago, in a language not now spoken; in a remote country, whose manners and customs were very different from ours. In all such cases, there will be obscurities and difficulties, arising entirely from the imperfection of our knowledge.

The Gospels do not purport to be regular histories of events, arranged in exact chronological order, but a selection of important facts, out of a much greater number left unnoticed. The time when, or the place where, these facts occurred, is of no consequence to the end contemplated by the evangelists. In their narratives, therefore, they have sometimes pursued the order of time; and in other cases, the arrangement has been suggested by the subject previously treated, or by some other circumstance.

In recording a miracle, the number of persons benefitted, is not of much consequence; the miracle is the same, whether sight be restored to one person, or two; or whether demons be expelled from one, or many. If one historian, intent on recording the extraordinary facts, selects the case of one person, which might, in. some accounts, be more remarkable; and another mentions two, there is no contradiction. If they had professed to give an accurate account of the number healed, there would be ground for this objection; but this was no part of the design of the evangelists.

If a writer, with a view of exhibiting the skill of an oculist, should mention a remarkable instance of sight being restored to a person who bad been long blind, it could not be fairly inferred from the narrative, that no other person received the same benefit, at that time; and, if, another person should give a distinct account of all the cases, there would be no contradiction between these witnesses. All the difference is, that one selects a prominent fact out of many; the other descends to all the particular.

There is no source of difficulty more usual, than the confounding of things which are distinct. The narratives of events truly distinct, may have so striking a similarity, that the cursory reader will be apt to confound them. It has been remarked by a learned man, [14] that if the two miracles of feeding the multitude, bad been mentioned by two different evangelists, each giving an account of one case, it would have been supposed by them that they were accounts of the same occurrence, and that the evangelists did not agree in their testimony: but in this case, both these miracles are distinctly related by the same evangelist, and distinctly referred to by Christ, in his conversation with his disciples. This confounding of distinct things is never more commonly done, than when a fact was attended with a great number of circumstances and occurrences, rapidly succeeding each other, and the historian mentions only a few out of many. This remark is fully verified with respect to Christ's resurrection. The narrative of all the evangelists is very concise. Few particulars are mentioned; and yet from the nature of the case, there must have been an extraordinary degree of agitation among the disciples; a great running from one part of Jerusalem to another, to tell the news; and a frequent paging to and from the sepulchre. It is not wonderful, therefore, that, as each evangelist mentions only a few of the accompanying occurrences; there should seem, at first view, to be some discrepancy in their accounts.

Companies of women are mentioned by each, and it is hastily taken for granted, that they were all the same; and the objector proceeds on the supposition, that these women all arrived at the sepulchre, at the same time, and that they continued together. He forgets to take into view, that the persons who might agree to meet at thé sepulchre, probably lived at very different distances from the place, and allows nothing for the agitation and distraction produced by the reports and visions of this interesting morning. But on this, as on several other subjects, we are indebted to the enemies of revelation for being the occasion of bringing forward able men, who have shed so much light on this part of the Gospel history, that even the appearance of discrepancy is entirely removed. [15]

The genealogy of Jesus Christ, as given by Matthew and Luke, has furnished to modern infidels much occasion of cavil; but it ought to be sufficient to silence these objectors, that the early enemies of Christianity made no objections on this ground. If one of these is the genealogy of Joseph and the other of Mary, there will be no discrepancy between them. Why it was proper to give the descent of Joseph, the husband of Mary, it is not now necessary to inquire. But on this whole subject, I would remark, that we are very little acquainted with the plan on which genealogical tables were constructed. It seems to have been a very intricate business, and it is not surprising that we should be at a loss to elucidate every difficulty.

Again, it is highly probable, that these lists were. taken from some genealogical tables of the tribe and family of the persons to whom they refer. Every family must have had access to such tables; on account of their inheritance. Public tables of acknowledged authority, would be far better for the purpose which the evangelists had in view, than new ones, even though these should have been more full and accurate. These genealogies had no other object than to prove that Jesus of Nazareth was a lineal descendant of David and Abraham; which purpose. is completely answered by them; and there are no difficulties which may not be accounted for by our ignorance of the subject.

Finally, it may be admitted, that some slight inaccuracies have crept into the copies of the New Testament, through the carelessness of transcribers. It is impossible for men to write the whole of a book, without making some mistakes; and if there be some small discrepancies, in the Gospels, with respect to names and numbers, they ought to be attributed to this cause.

VII. The witnesses of the miracles of Christ could have had no conceivable motive for propagating an imposture. That they were not themselves deceived is manifest from the nature of the facts, and from the full opportunity which they had of examining them. It is evident, therefore, that if the miracles recorded by them never existed, they were wilful impostors. They must have wickedly combined, to impose upon the world. But what motives could have influenced them to pursue such a course, we cannot imagine; or how men of low condition and small education, should have ever conceived it possible to deceive the world, in such a case, is equally inconceivable. These men had worldly interests, which it was natural for them to regard; but every thing of this kind, was fully relinquished. They engaged in an enterprise not only dangerous, but attended with certain and immediate ruin to all their worldly interests. They exposed themselves to the indignation of all authority, and to the outrageous fury of the multitude. They must have foreseen, that they would bring down upon themselves the vengeance of the civil and ecclesiastical powers, and that every species of suffering awaited them. Their leader was crucified, and what could they expect from declaring that he was alive, and had performed wonderful miracles? If they could have entertained any hopes of exemption from evils so apparent, experience must soon have convinced them, that they had engaged not only in a wicked, but most unprofitable undertaking. It was not long after they began their testimony, before they were obliged to endure unrelenting persecution from Jews and Gentiles. Could they have been influenced by a regard to fame? What renown could they expect from proclaiming a crucified man to be their master, and the object of all their hope and confidence? If this was their object, why did they give. all the glory to another who was. dead? But the fact is, that instead of fame, they met with infamy. No name was ever more derided and hated than that of Christian. They were vilified as the most contemptible miscreants that ever lived; as the refuse and offscouring of all things; as the pests and disturbers of society, and the enemies of the gods. They were pursued as outlaws, and punished for no other reason, but because they acknowledged themselves to be Christians. Would men persevere in propagating an imposture for such fame as this? It cannot be supposed that they expected their compensation in another world; for, the supposition is, that they were wilful impostors, who were, every day, asserting, in the most solemn manner, that the murderer or highway robber is influenced in the commission of his atrocious crimes, by the hope of a future reward.

The only alternative is, to suppose, that they were fanatics; as it is known, that men under the government of enthusiasm, contemn all the common considerations, which usually influence human conduct; and often act in a way totally unaccountable. This representation of enthusiasm is just, but it will not answer the purpose for which it is adduced. Enthusiasts are always. strongly persuaded of the truth of the religion which they wish to propagate; but these men, upon the hypothesis under consideration, knew that all which they said was false. Enthusiasm, and imposture are irreconcilable. It is true, that, what begins in enthusiasm, may end in imposture; but in. this case, the imposture must have been the beginning, as well as the end, of the whole business. There was no room for enthusiasm; all was imposture, if the facts reported, were not true. But the best evidence, that the evangelists were not wild fanatics, is derived front their writings. These are at the greatest remove from the ravings or reveries of enthusiasm. They are the most simple, grave, and dispassionate narratives, that ever were written. These books, certainly, were not the production of crazy fanatics. The writers are actuated by no frenzy; they give no indication of a heated imagination; they speak, uniformly, the language of "truth and soberness."

VIII. But if we could persuade ourselves, that the apostles might have been actuated by some unknown and inconceivable motive, to forge the- whole account of Christ's miracles; and were impelled by some unaccountable phrensy, to persevere, through all difficulties and sufferings, to propagate lies; yet, can we believe, that they could have found followers, in the very country, and in the very city, where the miracles were stated to have been performed?

When these accounts of stupendous and numerous miracles were published in Jerusalem where the apostles began their testimony, what would the people think? Would they not say, "These men bring strange things to our ears? They tell us of wonders wrought among us, of which we have never before heard. And they would not only have us to believe their incredible story, but forsake all. that we have, abandon our friends, and relinquish the religion of our fore-fathers, received from God: and not only so, but bring upon ourselves and families, the vengeance of those that rule over us, and the hatred and reproach of all men." Is it possible to believe, that one sane person, would have received their report?

Besides, the priests and rulers who had put Jesus to death, were deeply interested to prevent the circulation of such a story. It implicated them in a horrid crime. Would they not have exerted

## The Evidences of the Christian Religion

themselves to lay open the forgery, and would there have been the least difficulty in accomplishing the object, if the testimony of these witnesses had been false? The places of many of the miracles are recorded, and the names of the persons healed, or raised from the dead, mentioned. It was only one or two miles to the dwelling of Lazarus; how easy would it have been to prove that the story of his resurrection was a falsehood, had it not been a fact? Indeed, Jerusalem itself, and the temple, were the scenes of many of the miracles ascribed to Christ. As he spent much time in that city, it is presumable, that not a person residing there, could have been totally ignorant of facts which must have occupied the attention and excited the curiosity of every body. An imposture like this could never be successful, in such circumstances. The presence of an interested, inimical, and powerful body of men, would soon have put down every attempt at an imposition so gross and groundless. If the apostles had pretended, that at some remote period, or in some remote country, a man had performed miracles, they might have persuaded some weak and credulous persons; but they appealed to the people to whom they preached, as the witnesses of what they related. No more than a few weeks had elapsed after the death of Jesus, before this testimony was published in Jerusalem: and, notwithstanding all the opposition of those in authority, it was received, and multitudes willingly offered themselves as the disciples of him, whom they had recently crucified.

The success of the Gospel, under the circumstances of its first publication, is one of the most wonderful' effects recorded in history; and it is a fact beyond all dispute. In a little time, thousands of persons embraced the Christian religion, in Jerusalem, and in other parts of Judea. In heathen countries, its success was still more astonishing.

Churches were planted in all the principal cities of the Roman Empire, before half a century had elapsed from the resurrection of Christ. The fires of persecution raged; thousands and tens of thousands of unoffending Christians were put to death, in a cruel manner; yet this cause' seemed to prosper the more, so that it became a proverb, that "the blood of the martyrs was the seed of the Church." And it went on increasing and prevailing, until, in less than three centuries, it became the religion of the empire.

Learned infidels have in vain attempted to assign an adequate cause for this event, on natural principles. Gibbon, as has been before stated, exerted all his ingenuity to account for the progress and establishment of Christianity; but although he has freely indulged conjecture, and disregarded the testimony of Christians, his efforts have been unavailing. The account which he has given, is entirely unsatisfactory. Upon the deistical hypothesis, it is a grand revolution, without any adequate cause. That a few unlearned and simple men, mostly fishermen of Galilee, should have been successful in changing the religion of the world, without power or patronage, and employing no other weapons but persuasion, must, forever, remain an unaccountable thing, unless we admit the reality of miracles, and supernatural aid.

The argument from the rapid and extensive progress. of the Gospel may be estimated, if we consider the following circumstances:

1. The insufficiency of the instruments to accomplish such a work, without supernatural aid. They had neither the learning nor address to make such an impression on the minds of men, as was requisite, to bring about such a revolution.

2. The places in which the Gospel was first preached and had greatest success, furnish proof, that it could not have been propagated merely by human means. These were not obscure corners, remote from the lights of science, but the most populous and polished cities, where every species of the learning of the age was concentrated, and whither men of learning resorted. Damascus, Antioch, Ephesus, Corinth, Phillippi, and Rome, furnished the theatre for the first preachers of the Gospel. It is believed, that there was no conspicuous city, in the central part of the Roman, empire, in which a Christian church was not planted, before the death of the apostles. And it ought to be remembered, that this did not occur in a dark age, but in what is acknowledged by all, to be the most enlightened age of antiquity: it was the period which immediately succeeded the Augustan Age, so much, and so deservedly celebrated, for its classical authors. If the Gospel had been an imposture, its propagators would never have gone to such places, in the first instance; or if they had, they could not have escaped detection.

3. The obstacles to be overcome were great, and insurmountable by human effort. The people were all attached to the respective superstitions, in which they had been educated, and which were all adapted to retain their hold on corrupt minds. How difficult is it to obtain, even a hearing, from people in such circumstances, is manifest from the experience of all missionaries, in modern times. Philosophers, priests, and rulers, were combined against them. All that learning, eloquence, prejudice, interest, and power, could oppose to them, stood in their way.

4. It would have been impracticable for a few unlettered Jews to acquire the languages of all the nations, among whom the Gospel spread, in so short a time. They must have had the gift of tongues; or this conquest could never have been achieved. Besides, it ought to be remembered, that Jews were held in great contempt, by all the surrounding nations. A few persons of this nation, exhibiting a very mean

appearance, as must have been the case, would have called forth nothing but derision and contempt, in any of the large cities of the Empire. It is more unlikely that they should have been able to make many converts, than it would be now, for a few poor Jewish mechanics to proselyte to Judaism, vast multitudes, in all the principal cities of Europe and America. [16]

5. The terms of discipleship, which the apostles proposed, and the doctrines which they preached, were not adapted to allure and flatter the people, but must have been very repulsive to the minds of men.

6. Many Christians were cut off by persecution, but still Christianity made progress, and was extended in all directions. Because Christianity increased and flourished under bloody persecutions, many persons have adopted it as a maxim, that persecution has a tendency to promote any cause; than which it is difficult to conceive of any thing more contrary to common sense and experience. In most cases, by cutting off the leaders of a party, however furious their fanaticism, the cause will decline, and soon become extinct. The increase of Christianity, under ten bloody persecutions, can only be accounted for, by supposing, that God by his grace on the hearts of men, persuaded them to embrace the truth, and inspired them with more than heroic fortitude, in suffering for the sake of their religion.

IX. The apostles and many of the primitive Christians, attested the truth by martyrdom. They sealed their testimony with their blood. To this argument it is sometimes answered, that men may suffer martyrdom for a false as well as a true religion; and that, in fact, men have been willing to die for opinions, in direct opposition to each other. While this is admitted, it does not affect the argument now adduced. All, that dying for an opinion can prove, (and of this it is the best possible evidence,) is, the sincerity of the witnesses But in the case before us, the sincerity of the witnesses proves the facts in question; for we have seen, that they could not themselves have been deceived. Every martyr had the opportunity of knowing the truth of the facts on which Christianity was founded; and by suffering death in attestation of them, he has given the most impressive testimony that can he conceived. [17]

The sufferings of the primitive Christians, for their religion, were exceedingly great, and are attested by heathen, as well as Christian writers. It is a circumstance of great importance, in this argument, that they could at once have escaped all their torments, by renouncing Christianity. To bring them to this, was the sole object of their persecutors; and, uniformly, it was put to their choice, to offer sacrifice or incense to the heathen gods, or be tormented. One word would have been sufficient to deliver them; one easy action would have restored them to worldly comforts and honors: But they steadfastly adhered to their profession. Some, indeed, were overcome by the cruelty of their persecutors; but was it ever beard that any of them confessed that there was any fraud or imposture, among them? So far from it, that they, whose courage had failed them in the trying hour, were commonly deep penitents on account of their weakness, all the rest of their days. Let it be remembered, that no person suffered for Christianity through necessity. Every martyr made a voluntary sacrifice of himself, to maintain the truth, and to preserve a good conscience.

There is yet another light in which these sufferings of the primitive Christians ought to be viewed. It is the temper with which they endured every kind of torment. Here again is a problem for the deist to solve. Persons of all ages, of all conditions of life, and of both sexes, exhibited under protracted and cruel torments, a fortitude, a patience, a meekness, a spirit of charity and forgiveness, a cheerfulness, yea, often a triumphant joy, of which there are no examples to be found in the history of the world. They rejoiced when they were arrested; cheerfully bid adieu to their nearest and dearest relatives; gladly embraced the stake; welcomed the wild beasts let loose to devour them; smiled on the horrible apparatus by which their sinews were to be stretched, and their bones dislocated and broken; uttered no complaint; gave no indication of pain when their bodies were enveloped in flames; and when condemned to die, begged of their friends to interpose no obstacle to their felicity, (for such they esteemed martyrdom,) not even by prayers for their deliverance. [18] What more than human fortitude watt this? By what spirit were these despised and persecuted people sustained? What natural principles, in the human constitution, can satisfactorily account for such superiority to pain and death? Could attachment to an impostor inspire them with such feelings? No; it was the promised presence of the risen Jesus which upheld them, and filled them with assurance and joy. It was the Paraclete, promised by their Lord, who poured into their hearts a peace and joy so complete, that they were scarcely sensible of the wounds inflicted on their bodies.

Proud and obstinate men may, for aught I know, suffer death for what they are secretly convinced is not true; but that multitudes, of all conditions, should joyfully suffer for what they knew to be an imposture, is impossible. Tender women, and venerable old men, were among the most conspicuous of the martyrs of Jesus. They loved not their lives unto the death, and having given their testimony and sealed it with their blood, they are now clothed in white robes, and bear palms in their hands, and sing the song of Moses and the Lamb. Blessed martyrs, they have rested from their labors, and their works have followed them!

X. The last particular which I shall mention, to set the testimony of the witnesses to the miracles of the Gospel in its true light, is, that there is no counter testimony. These witnesses have never been confronted and contradicted by others. Whatever force or probability their declarations are entitled to, from the circumstances of the case, and from the evidences which we possess of their integrity and intelligence, suffers no deduction, on account of other persons giving a different testimony.

The Jewish priests and rulers did, indeed, cause to be circulated, a story, relative to the dead body of Christ, contrary to the testimony of the apostles, which has been handed down to us by the evangelists. They hired the soldiers to report., that Christ's disciples had come by night, and stolen the body, while they slept--a story too absurd and inconsistent to require a moment's refutation. But as the body was gone out of their possession; they could not, perhaps, have invented any thing more plausible. It proved nothing, however, except that the body was removed while the soldiers slept, and for aught they could testify, might have risen from the dead, according to the testimony of the apostles.

Deists sometimes demand the testimony of the enemies, as well as the friends of Christianity. To which I would reply, that the silence of enemies, is all that can reasonably be expected from them. That they should come forward, voluntarily, with testimony in favor of a religion, which, through prejudice, or worldly policy, they opposed, could not reasonably be expected. Now, since they would have contradicted these facts, if it had been in their power, their not doing so, furnishes the strongest negative evidence, which we can possess. And no other evidence than that which is negative, or merely incidental, ought to be expected from the enemies of the Gospel; unless, like Paul, they were convinced by the evidence exhibited to them. But no denial of the reality of the miracles of Christ has reached us from any quarter. As far as we have any accounts, there is no reason to think, that they were ever denied by his most implacable enemies. They said, that he performed his works by the help of Beelzebub. The first heathen writers against Christianity, did not dare to deny Christ's miracles. Neither Celsus, Porphyry, Hierocles, nor Julian, pretend, that these facts were entirely false; for they attempted to account for them. The Jewish Rabbies, in the Talmud, acknowledge these miracle`, and pretend that they were wrought by magic, or by the power of the venerable name of Jehovah, called, tertragrammaton, which they ridiculously pretend, Jesus stole out of the temple, and by which they say he performed wonderful works.

From what has been said, I trust it is sufficiently manifest, that we have such testimony for the miracles of the New Testament, as will render them credible, in the view of all impartial persons. We have shown that the miracles recorded are real miracles;--that. they were performed in an open and public manner;--that the witnesses could not possibly have been deceived themselves;--that enemies had every opportunity and motive for disproving the facts if they had not been true;--that there is every evidence of sincerity and honesty in the evangelists;--that the epistles of the apostles furnish strong collateral proof of the same facts;--that all Christians from the beginning, must have .believed in these miracles, and they must, therefore, be considered competent witnesses;--that none of the. witnesses could have any motive to deceive;--that they never could have succeeded in imposing such a fraud on the world, if they could have attempted it;--that it would have been the easiest thing in the world, for the Jewish Rulers to have silenced such reports if they had been false;--that the commencement of preaching. at Jerusalem, and the success of Christianity there, cannot be accounted for, on any other principles, than the truth of the miracles;--that the conduct of the apostles in going to the most enlightened countries and cities, and their success in those places, can never be reconciled with the idea that they were ignorant impostors;--that the astonishing progress of the Gospel, in the midst of opposition and persecution, and the extraordinary temper of the primitive Christians, under sufferings of the most cruel kind, can only be accounted for, on the supposition of a full persuasion of the truth of the facts, and that this persuasion is proof of their reality;--and, finally, that no contrary evidence exists: but that even the early enemies of Christianity have been obliged to admit, that such miracles were performed.

Now, when all these things are fairly and fully considered, is it not reasonable to conclude, that it is more probable that miracles should have been performed, than that such a body of testimony, so corroborated by circumstances, and by effects reaching to our own times, should be false?

If all this testimony is false, we may call in question all historical testimony whatever; for what facts ever have been so fully attested?

But why should this testimony he rejected? No reason has ever been assigned, except that the facts, were miraculous; but we have shown, that it is not unreasonable to expect miracles in such a case; and that miracles are capable of satisfactory proof from testimony. It is, therefore, a just conclusion, That the Miracles of the Gospel are credible.

## Footnotes:

7. See Pascal's Thoughts.
8. Decline and fall of the Roman Empire, c. iv., & xvi.
9. Mr. Roberts.
10. See Lardner's Heathen Testimonies.
11. See Lord Lyttleton's Conversion of Paul.

12. There is a remarkable testimony to the extraordinary character and works of Jesus Christ, in Josephus, which has been rejected as spurious by modern critics; not for want of external evidence, for it is found in all the oldest and best MSS., but principally because it is conceived, that Josephus being a Jew, and a Pharisee, never could have given such a testimony in favor of one is whom he did not believe.

13. See Dr. Channing's Dudleian Lecture.
14. Dr. Macknight.
15. See West on the Resurrection; Townson; Macknight; Ditton; Sherlock; &c.
16. See Dr. S. S. Smith's Lectures on the Evidences of Christianity.
17. See Addison's Evidences.
18. See the Epistles of Ignatius and Polycarp.

# CHAPTER VIII – THE BIBLE CONTAINS PREDICTIONS OF EVENTS, WHICH NO HUMAN SAGACITY COULD HAVE FORESEEN, AND WHICH HAVE BEEN EXACTLY AND REMARKABLY ACCOMPLISHED

THE subject of prophecy is so extensive, and the difficulty of presenting, with brevity, the argument which it furnishes, so great, that if I had not determined to give a general outline of the evidences of revelation, I should have omitted this topic, as one to to which justice cannot be done, in so short an essay.

But, I would not be understood as intimating, that the evidence from prophecy is of an inferior kind. So far from believing this to be the fact, I am persuaded, that whoever will take the pains to examine the subject thoroughly, will find that this source of evidence for the truth of revelation, is exceeded by no other, in the firmness of conviction which it is calculated to produce. Prophecy possesses, as a proof of divine revelation, some advantages which axe peculiar. For the proof of miracles we must have recourse to ancient testimony; but the fulfilling of prophecy may fall under our own observation, or may be conveyed to us by living witnesses. The evidence of miracles cannot, in any case, become stronger than it was at .first; but that of prophecy is continually increasing, and will go on increasing, until the whole scheme of predictions are fulfilled. The mere publication of a prediction furnishes no decisive evidence, that it is a revelation from God: it is the accomplishment which completes the proof. As prophecies have been fulfilled in every age, and are still in a course of being fulfilled; and as some most remarkable predictions remain to be accomplished, it is plain, from the nature of the case, that this proof will continue to increase in strength.

It deserves to be well weighed, that any one prediction which has been fulfilled, is, of itself, a complete evidence of divine revelation; or to speak more properly, is itself a revelation. For, certainly, no one but God himself can foretell distant future events which depend entirely on the purpose of Him, "who worketh all things after the council of his own will."

If then, we can adduce one prophecy, the accomplishment of which cannot be doubted, we have established the principle, that a revelation has been given; and if in one instance, and to one person, the probability is strong, that he is not the only person, who has been favored with such a communication.

The remark, which is frequently made, that most prophecies are obscure, and the meaning very uncertain, will not affect the evidence arising from such as are perspicuous, and of which the accomplishment is exact. There are good reasons, why these future events should sometimes be wrapped up in the covering of strong figures and symbolical language; so that often the prophet himself, probably, did not understand the meaning of the prediction which he uttered. It was not intended, that they should be capable of being dearly interpreted, until the key was furnished, by the completion. If these observations are just, the study (of the prophecies will become more and more interesting, every day; and they will shed more and more light on the truth of the Scriptures.

What I shall attempt at present, and all that is compatible with the narrow limits of this discourse, will be to exhibit a few remarkable predictions, and refer to the events, in which they have been fulfilled. They who wish for further satisfaction, will find it, in the perusal of Bishop Newton's excellent Dissertations on the prophecies, to which I acknowledge myself indebted for a considerable part of what is contained in this chapter.

The first prophecies which I will produce; are those of Moses, respecting the Jews. They are recorded, principally, in the xxvi. chapter of Leviticus, and in the xxviii. chapter of Deutoronomy; of which, the following predictions deserve our attention.

1. The Lord shall bring, a nation against thee from afar, from the end of the earth, as swift as the eagle flieth; a nation whose tongue thou shalt not understand. This prophecy had an accomplishment, both in the invasion of Judea by the Chaldeans, and by the Romans; but more especially, the latter.

*Archibald Alexander, D. D.*

Jeremiah, when predicting the invasion of the Chaldeans, uses nearly the same language as Moses. Lo, I will bring a nation upon you from afar, O house of Israel, saith the Lord, it is an ancient nation, a nation whose language thou knowest not. [19] --And again, Our persecutors are swifter than the eagles of the heaven. [20]

But with still greater propriety may it be said, that the Romans were a nation from afar; the rapidity of whose conquests resembled the eagle's flight; the standard of whose armies was au eagle; and whose language was unknown to the Jews.

The enemies of the Jews are also characterized as a nation of fierce countenance, who shall not regard the person of the old, nor show favor to the young. Which was an exact description of the Chaldeans. It is said, 2 Chron. xxxvi. 17, that God brought upon the Jews, the king of the Chaldees, who slew their young men with the sword in the house of their sanctuary, and had no compassion upon young man or maiden, old man, or him that stooped for age. Such also were the Romans. Josephus informs us, that when Vespasian came to Gadara, "he slew all, man by man, the Romans showing mercy to no age." The like was done at Gamala.

2. It was predicted, also, that their cities should be besieged and taken. And he shall besiege thee in all thy gates, until thy high and fenced walls come down, wherein thou trustedst. This was fulfilled when Shalmaneser, king of Assyria, came against Samaria, and besieged it: [21] when Sennacherib came up against all the fenced cities of Judah; and when Nebuchadnezzar took Jerusalem and burned the temple, and broke down the walls of Jerusalem round about. [22] The Jews had great confidence in the strength of the fortifications of Jerusalem. And Tacitus, as well as Josephus, describes it as a very strong place; yet it was often besieged and taken, before its final destruction by Titus.

In their sieges they were to suffer much by famine, in the straitness wherewith their enemies should distress them. Accordingly, at Samaria, during the the siege, there was a great famine, so that an asses head was sold for four score pieces of silver. [23]

And when Jerusalem was besieged by Nebuchadnezzar, the famine prevailed in the city, and there was no bread for the people of the land. [24] And in the siege of the same city by the Romans, there was a most distressing famine. [25]

It was foretold, that in these famines, women should eat their own children. Ye shall eat, says Moses, the flesh of your sons and of your daughters. And again, thou shalt eat the fruit of thine own body. [26] The tender and delicate woman among you, who would not adventure to set the sole of her foot upon the ground, for delicateness and tenderness--she shall eat her children for want of all things, secretly in the siege and straitness, wherewith thine enemies shall distress thee in thy gates. This extraordinary prediction was fulfilled, six hundred years after it. was spoken, in the siege of Samaria, by the king of Syria; when two women agreed together to give up their children to be eaten; and one of them was eaten accordingly. [27] It was fulfilled again, nine hundred years after Moses, in the siege of Jerusalem, by the Chaldeans. The hands of the pitiful women, says Jeremiah, have sodden their own children. [28] And again, fifteen hundred years after the time of Moses, when Jerusalem was besieged by the Romans, Josephus informs us, of a noble woman killing and eating her own sucking child, and when she had eaten half; she secreted the other part for another meal.

3. Great numbers of the Jews were to be destroyed. And ye shall be left few in number, whereas ye were as the stars of heaven for multitude. In the siege of Jerusalem, by Titus, it is computed that eleven hundred thousand persons perished, by famine, pestilence, and sword. Perhaps, since the creation of the world, so many persons never perished in any one siege as this.

The occasion of so great a multitude of people being found at Jerusalem, was, that the siege commenced about the celebration of the passover; and the people throughout the adjacent country, took refuge in Jerusalem, at the approach of the Roman army.

Moses also predicted, that the Jews should be carried back to Egypt, and sold as slaves, for a very low price, and described the method of their conveyance thither; And the Lord shall bring thee into Egypt again with ships, where you shall be sold unto your enemies for bondmen and bondwomen, and no man shall buy you. Josephus informs us, that when the city was taken, the captives who were above seventeen years of age, were sent to the works in Egypt: but so little care was taken of these captives, that eleven thousand of them perished for want. There is every probability, though the historian does not mention the fact, that they were conveyed to Egypt, in ships, as the Romans had then a fleet in the Mediterranean. The market was so overstocked, that there were no purchasers, and they were sold for the merest trifle.

4. It is, moreover, predicted in this wonderful prophecy of Moses, that the Jews should be extirpated from their own land, and dispersed among all nations. And ye shall be plucked from off the land whither thou goest to possess it. And the Lord shall scatter thee among all people, from one end of the earth, even unto the other.

How remarkably this has been fulfilled, is known to all. The ten tribes were first carried away from their own land, by the King of Assyria; and next, the two other tribes were carried captive to Babylon; and, finally, when the Romans took away their place and nation, their dispersion was

47

*The Evidences of the Christian Religion*
complete.

Afterwards, Adrian forbade the Jews, by a public edict, to set foot in Jerusalem, on pain of death; or even to approach the country around it. In the time Of Tertullian and Jerome, they were prohibited from entering into Judea. And from that day to this, the number of Jews, in the holy land, has been very small. They are still exiles from their own land, and are found scattered through almost every country on the globe.

5. But it is foretold, that, notwithstanding their dispersion, they should not be totally destroyed, but should exist still, as a distinct people. And yet for all Mat, when they be in the land of their enemies, I will not cast them away, neither will I abhor them; to destroy them utterly, and to break my covenant with them. "What a marvellous thing is this," says Bishop Newton, "that after so many wars, battles, and sieges; after so many rebellions, massacres, and persecutions; after so many years of captivity, slavery, and misery; they are not destroyed utterly, and though scattered among all people, yet subsist a distinct people by themselves! where is any thing like this to be found in all the histories, and in all the nations under the sun?"

The prophecy goes on to declare, that they should he; every where, in an uneasy condition; and should not rest long, in any one place. And among these nations shalt thou find no ease, neither shall the sole of thy foot have rest. How exactly this has been verified, in the case of this unhappy people, even unto this day, is known to all. There is scarcely a country in Europe, from which they have not been banished, at one time or another. To say nothing of many previous scenes of bloodshed and banishment, of the most shocking kind, through which, great multitudes of this devoted people passed, in Germany, France, and Spain, in the thirteenth and fourteenth centuries; eight hundred thousand Jews, are said by the Spanish historian, to have been banished from Spain, by Ferdinand and Isabella. And how often, when tolerated by government, they have suffered by the tumults of the people, it is impossible to enumerate.

The prophet declares, That they should be oppressed and crushed alway; that their sons and their daughters should be given to another people; that they should be mad for the sight of their eyes, which they should see. Nothing has been more common in all countries, where the Jews has resided, than to fine, fleece, and oppress them at will; and in Spain and Portugal, their children have been taken from them, by order of the government, to be educated in the Popish religion. The instances, also, in which their oppressions have driven them to madness and desperation, are too numerous to be here stated in detail.

6. Finally, it is foretold by Moses, That they should become an astonishment, a proverb, and a by-word, among all nations; and that their plagues should be wonderful, even great plagues, and of long continuance. In every country the Jews are hated and despised. They have been literally a proverb, and a by-word. Mohammedans, Heathens, and Christians, however they differ in other things, have been agreed in vilifying, abusing, and persecuting the Jews. Surely, the judgments visited on this peculiar people, have been wonderful, and of long continuance. For nearly eighteen hundred years, they have been in this miserable state of banishment, dispersion, and persecution.

"What nation," says the distinguished writer already quoted, "hath subsisted as a distinct people in their own country, so long, as these have done in their dispersion, into all countries? And what a standing miracle is this exhibited to the view and observation of the whole world!"--"Here are instances of prophecies delivered above three thousand years ago, and yet., as we see, fulfilling in the world, at this very time; and what stronger proof can we desire of the divine legation of Moses? How these instances may affect others, I know not, but for myself, I must acknowledge, they not only convince, but amaze and astonish me beyond expression."

The prophecies, in the Old Testament, concerning Nineveh, Babylon, Tyre, and Egypt, are highly deserving our attention; not only because they are expressed in the plainest language, but because the fulfilment of them has not been confined to one age, but has continued for thousands of years, and is as remarkable at this time, as in any former period; but the narrow limits which we have prescribed to ourselves, forbid our entering on this subject.

It may be safely affirmed, however, that the more closely these prophecies are compared with subsequent events--events altogether improbable in themselves, and of a truly extraordinary character--the more dearly will the impartial and discerning see in them, marks of a divine origin.

The prophecy of Isaiah respecting Cyrus, by name, two hundred years before he was born, is very clear, and no less remarkable.

"That saith of Cyrus, he is my shepherd and shall perform all my pleasure, even saying to Jerusalem, thou shalt be built, and to the temple, thy fonndation shall be laid. Thus saith the Lord to Cyrus Isis anointed, to Cyrus whose right hand I have holden, to subdue nations before him, and I will loose the loins of kings to open before him the two leaved gates, that shall not be shut. I will go before thee and make the crooked places straight; I will break in pieces the gates of brass, and will cut in sunder the bars of iron, and I will give thee the treasures of darkness, and hidden riches of secret places, that thou mayest know, that I, the Lord, which call thee by thy name, am the God of Israel. For Jacob, my servant's sake, and Israel mine elect, I have even called thee by thy name, I have surnamed thee, though thou hast not known me. [29] "

We are informed by Josephus, that after Cyrus had got possession of Babylon, this prophecy was shown to him; and that he was struck with admiration at the manifest divinity of the writing. Besides the name of Cyrus, two extraordinary events are foretold; the capture of Babylon, with its iron bars and gates of brass, and containing hidden treasures;--and the restoration of the Jews, and the rebuilding of their city and temple. And every thing is so plain, that there is no possibility of evading the. force of the argument.

The prophecies recorded in the book of Daniel; also, are very wonderful. There we have described, the rise and fall of four successive monarchies, or empires; also, a .prophecy concerning the conquests of Alexander the Great, and concerning his successors, embracing so many particulars, that. it assumes the appearance of a history of the events which it predicts. Porphyry, an early and learned opposer of Christianity, was so struck with the coincidence between the predictions, and the history of the events by which they are fulfilled; that he declared that the prophecy must have been written after the events occurred. The infidel can make no complaint of obscurity here, as he commonly does, when prophecies are adduced; the objection now is, that the prediction is too manifest, and circumstantial. This objection of Porphyry, induced Jerome to use the following pertinent language: "Cujus impugnatio testimonium veritatis est. Tanta enim dictorum fides fuit, ut propheta incredulis hominibus non videatur futura dixisse, sed narrasse, præterita." The meaning of which is, "This objection is a testimony to the truth; for such is the perspicuity of the language, that the prophet, in the opinion of infidel men, seems rather to be narrating past events, than predicting those which are future."

It will be sufficient to observe, that there is not the least foundation for this opinion of Porphyry, that the book of Daniel was written after the time of Antiochus Epiphanes. Josephus relates, that the prophecies of Daniel were shown to Alexander the Great, when he visited Jerusalem; and that this was the reason of his granting so many privileges to the Jewish people. However this may be, Daniel is spoken of in the first book of Maccabees; and Josephus himself reckons him among the greatest of prophets. And if they had been written at that late period, they never could have found a place in the Jewish canon, as the prophecies of Daniel. These prophecies are also recognised and quoted by Jesus Christ, as the productions of Daniel.

The prophecies which relate to the Messiah are so numerous and interesting, and involve so much critical discussion, that to exhibit them in their proper light, a volume would scarcely be sufficient. I must, therefore, be contented to refer to the most remarkable of these predictions, in a very brief and general way.

1. It is plain, from a cursory perusal of the Old Testament, that frequent intimations are given of the coming of a remarkable personage. From these, the Jewish nation have been led, in all ages, to entertain the expectation of a Messsiah; and from them, the idea of a distinguished person who was to proceed from Judea, seems to have pervaded the surrounding nations. Some of the passages of Scripture, on which this opinion was founded, were, the promise of The seed of the woman;--The seed of Abraham in whom all nations should be blessed;--The Shiloh who was to come out of Judah, before the dominion of that tribe should depart.--The prophet like unto Moses, whom the Lord would raise up;--The king whom the Lord would set upon his holy hill;--The priest after the order of Melchisedek; The anointed One, or Messiah--The righteous branch--The corner stone--The desire of all nations--The Shepherd of Israel.

2. The time of the arrival of the Messiah is designated in prophecy. He was to come before the sceptre departed from Judah, at the end of seventy prophetic weeks, or four hundred and ninety years, from the time of the going forth of the command, to restore and build Jerusalem, and while the second temple was yet standing.

3. The place of his birth, and the family from which he was to descend, were also explicitly mentioned in prophecy. From the evangelical history, and from the acknowledgment of the Jews, it is evident, that they well knew, that the Messiah was to be born at Bethlehem, and to be of the family of David:

4. Things of an apparently contradictory nature: are predicted concerning the Messiah. At one time he is represented as a king and conqueror, whose dominion would be co-extensive with the earth, and' who would flourish in righteousness and peace forever; at another, he is exhibited as one despised and rejected; a man of sorrow and grief; as wounded and bruised;--as cut of out of the land of the; and as pouring out his soul unto death. These apparently irreconcilable characters, led the Jews at one time, to entertain the opinion, that two Messiahs were predicted; the one a triumphant conqueror; the other a persecuted and patient sufferer.. But, however great the apparent inconsistency, there is an exact accomplishment of both characters, in Jesus of Nazareth. And, certainly, the same cannot be said of any other person who ever lived.

5. It is predicted of the Messiah, that he should be a light to the Gentiles; and that under his administration, the face of the world should be changed; and that peace and righteousness should

prevail. Although this prophecy is only in part fulfilled, yet so much has been accomplished in the call of numerous Gentile nations to the standard of the Messiah, and in the benign and salutary influence of Christianity, that we must conclude that it was uttered under the influence of inspiration.

6. It was not only predicted, that Messiah should be cut off, but it is expressly stated, that he should die as a vicarious sacrifice--an expiatory victim for sin and transgression. "Thou shalt make his soul an offering for sin."

For the fulfilling of these predictions, I need only refer to the New Testament.

That there is a remarkable coincidence between the language of the prophets and the history of the evangelists, cannot be denied, however it may be accounted for. The fifty-third chapter of Isaiah has a counterpart in the sufferings and death of Christ, which has forced conviction on the minds of many unbelievers.

But there are also many particular facts and circumstances foretold respecting the Messiah, which it may be proper, briefly to mention. His forerunner, John the Baptist, is predicted by Isaiah and Malachi. His miracles, his uncomplaining meekness and tranquil submission under cruel sufferings, by Isaiah. His riding on an ass, and a colt the foal of an ass;--his being pierced where the wound should be visible.;--his being sold for thirty pieces of silver, which should be, appropriated to buy the Potter's Field, by Zechariah. It is predicted in the Psalms, that they would part his raiment and cast lots for his vesture; and that vinegar would be given to him to drink. The very words, also, which he uttered on the cross, when forsaken of God, are set down in the xxii. Psalm, v. 1.

It was also predicted in the Law of Moses, by an expressive type, that not a bone of Icing should be broken; the fulfilment of which was wonderful, since the legs of both those crucified with him were broken.

Isaiah foretold, that he should make his grave with the wicked, and with the rich in his death, which was literally accomplished, when Jesus Christ was suspended on the between two thieves; and when he was taken down from the cross, by a rich man, and buried by him, in his own new tomb.

The most of these particulars were fulfilled by the free actions of the enemies of Jesus, who had no idea that they were fulfilling any divine prophecy. It is impossible, that so many circumstances, literally predicted, should have been fulfilled by a mere fortuitous concurrence.

The truth is, the whole ritual law is a prophecy of Jesus. To him the whole Old Testament dispensation had reference. The Law, the Psalms, and the Prophets, all testify of him. As said the angel to St. John, "The testimony of Jesus is the spirit of prophecy."

Christ himself delivered, while upon earth, many clear and remarkable prophecies. Most of his parables have a prophetic character, and in a striking manner represented the Gospel, the rejection of the Jews, the calling of the Gentiles, and the future condition of the Church. He also foretold, in express words, the treatment which his followers should receive from the world, the treachery of Judas Iscariot, the conduct of Peter in denying him three times in one night, and the particular circumstances and exact manner of his own death, and also his resurrection on the third day. But I must pass over all these, at present, and confine my attention to that astonishing prophecy, which Jesus delivered to his disciples on Mount Olivet, concerning the utter destruction of the temple of Jerusalem, and of the whole Jewish, nation. This prediction was uttered about forty years before the events occurred, to which it relates; and was recorded by St. Matthew, according to the common opinion of early writers, thirty, or at least twenty years before it was fulfilled. The same was recorded by Mark, and Luke, a few years after the writing of Matthew's Gospel, but several years before the occurrence of those prodigious things, which are foretold in it. The testimony of antiquity is, that both these evangelists were dead before the invasion of Judea, by the Romans. John was the only one of the evangelists, or perhaps of the apostles, who lived to witness the fulfilling of his Lord's prophecy; and it is remarkable, that in his Gospel, this subject is never mentioned.

Let it be remembered, that when this prophecy was delivered by our Saviour, there was not the least human probability of such an event, as the destruction of Jerusalem. The Jews were in a state of profound peace; and the power of the Romans was such, that it could not have been conjectured, that one small nation would think of rebelling against them.

The words of this prophecy may be read in the xxiv. chapter of the Gospel of Matthew; also in the xiii. chapter of the Gospel of Mark; and in the xix. and xxi chapters of the Gospel of Luke.

I will first collect into one view, all the most remarkable particulars of this prophecy, and then show how they were fulfilled. The predictions relate, 1. to the signs and precursors of the desolation of the holy city; 2. to the circumstances of its siege and capture; and 3. to the consequences of this tremendous catastrophe.

1. The signs and precursors of this event were to be, false Christs,--seditions and wars,--famines, pestilences, earthquakes, and extraordinary appearances in the heavens;--the persecution of Christians;--the apostacy of professors; and the great want of charity and depravation of morals among the people.

2. The circumstances of this tremendous judgment of heaven, are such as these: the event should occur before the existing generation had completely passed away;--that it should be brought on by a war

waged against the Jews, by a heathen nation, bearing idolatrous ensigns:--that Jerusalem should be utterly destroyed, and the temple so completely demolished, that one stone of that. sacred edifice, should not be left on another:--that multitudes should perish by the sword:--that great numbers should be carried away captives:--that the distress should exceed any thing, which had ever occurred in the world;--and that the divine wrath should be manifest in all these calamities, as it is called the day of vengeance; and it is said, that there should be wrath against the people.

3. The consequences of the destruction of the temple of Jerusalem, as predicted by Christ, were to be, the dispersion of the Jews through all the nations;--the total overthrow of the Jewish commonwealth, which is expressed by the prophetic symbols of the sun being darkened, the moon not giving her light, and the stars falling from heaven;--the rejection of the Jews, and the calling of the Gentiles;--the rising of false prophets, and false Messiahs;--the extent and continuance of these judgments on the Jewish nation; with some intimation of their restoration. The escape of the Christians from these calamities, is also foretold, and directions given for their flight; and on their account, it is promised, that those days should be shortened; and finally, it is predicted that the Gospel should be preached among alt nations.

Let us now proceed to inquire, in what manner these numerous and extraordinary predictions were accomplished; and we cannot but remark, that it seems to have been ordered, specially, by Providence, that the history of the series of events by which this prophecy was fulfilled, should be written by a man who was not a Christian; and who was an eye-witness of the facts, which he records. I allude to the Jewish historian, Josephus, who is an author of high respectability, and of great value to the cause of Christianity.

1. In regard to false Christs, of which the prophecy speaks so emphatically, we learn from the historian, just mentioned, that impostors and magicians drew multitudes after them, into the wilderness, promising to show them signs and wonders, some of whom became deranged, and others were punished by Felix, the procurator. One a these impostors was, that Egyptian, spoken of in the Acts of the Apostles, who drew multitudes of people after him to Mount Olivet, promising that he would cause the walls of Jerusalem to fall down at his word.

Theudas was another, who pretended to be a prophet, and gave out that he would divide the waters of Jordan; but he was quickly routed by Cuspius Fadus, and all his followers scattered. The impostor himself was taken alive, and his head cut off, and brought to Jerusalem. In the reign of Nero, and during the time that Felix was procurator of Judea, impostors arose in such numbers, that the historian informs us, "many of them were apprehended and killed every day."

There were also, at this time, great commotions, and horrible seditions and wars, in various places; as at Cesarea, Alexandria, and Babylonia. There were great contentions between the Jews and Samaritans; and also between the Jews and people of other nations, who dwelt in the same cities with them. Both Josephus and Philo, give a particular account of these disturbances, in which multitudes of the people were slain.

Famines, pestilences, and earthquakes, are mentioned by Suetonius, and by several other profane historians, who are cited by Eusebius, by Josephus, by Tacitus, and by Seneca.

That prodigies were frequent, is expressly asserted, by Josephus and Tacitus. The former declares that a star hung over the city like a sword, for a whole year;--that at the ninth hour of the night, a bright light shone round the altar and the temple, so that for the space of half an hour, it appeared to be bright day;--that the eastern gate of the temple, which it required twenty men to shut, and which was fastened by strong bars and bolts, opened of its own accord:--that before sun set, there was seen in the clouds, the appearance of chariots and armies fighting;--that at the feast of Pentecost, while the priests were going into the inner temple, a voice was heard, as of a multitude, saying, Let us depart hence. And what affected the people more than any thing else, was, that four years before the war began, a countryman came to Jerusalem, at the feast of Tabernacles, and ran up and own, crying day and night, "A voice from the east, a voice from the west, a voice from the four winds, a voice against Jerusalem and the temple. Wo! Wo! to Jerusalem?" It was in vain that by stripes and torture the magistrates attempted to restrain him: he continued crying, especially at the public festivals, for seven years and five months, and yet never grew hoarse, nor appeared to be weary: until during the siege, while he was crying on the wall, a stone struck him, and killed him instantly. Tacitus, the Roman historian, joins his testimony to that of Josephus:--"Armies," says he, "were seen engaged in the heavens, the glittering of arms was observed; and suddenly the fire from the clouds illuminated the temple; the doors of the inner temple were suddenly thrown open; and a voice more than human was heard proclaiming, the gods are departing: and at the same time, the motion of their departure was perceived." Men may form what judgment they please of these narratives; but one thing is certain, that the minds of men were, about this time, much agitated and terrified with what appeared to them to be prodigies. There were, fearful sights, and great signs from heaven.

2. The circumstances accompanying the siege and rapture of the city, were as exactly foretold, as the preceding signs. "The abomination of desolation," spoken of by Daniel the prophet, was nothing else than the Roman armies, whose ensign was an eagle perched upon a spear: which ensigns were

worshipped, as divinities. These stood where "they ought not," when they were planted, not only in the holy land, but on the consecrated spot, where the temple had stood. But the Christians had been warned, at the first appearance of this desolating abomination, immediately to betake themselves to flight; which they did, and instead of going into the city, they retired to Pella, beyond Jordan.

The distress of the Jews, within the city, during the siege, where two or three millions of people were crowded into a narrow space, almost exceeds belief. What with their continual battles with the Romans; what with intestine feuds and tumults; and what with famine and pestilence, the sufferings which they endured, cannot now be conceived. No such distress was ever experienced by any people, before or since.

Jerusalem was hemmed in on all sides, by the besieging army, and notwithstanding the great strength of its fortifications, was taken. Although Titus had given express orders, that the temple should be preserved; yet the mouth of the Lord, had declared, that it should be otherwise: and, accordingly, it was burnt to the ground, and the very foundation dug up by the soldiers, with the hope of finding hidden treasures. After the city had been destroyed, Titus ordered the whole space to be levelled like a field; so that a person approaching the place, would hardly suspect that it had ever been inhabited.

The number slain in the war has already been mentioned; to which we may now add, that the captives amounted to ninety-seven thousand. Josephus, in relating these events, adopts a language remarkably similar to that used by Christ, in the prophecy. "The calamities of all people," says he, "from the creation of the world, if they be compared with those suffered by the Jews, will be found to be far surpassed by them." The words of Christ are; There shall be great tribulation, such as was not from the beginning of the world to this time; no, nor ever shall be.

That these unparalleled calamities proceeded from the vengeance of heaven, against a people whose iniquities were full, was not only acknowledged by Josephus, but by Titus, the Roman general. After taking a survey of the city, the height of the towers and walls, the magnitude of the stones, and the strength of the bands by which they were held together, he broke out into the following exclamation: "By the help of God, we have brought this war to a conclusion. It was God, who drew out the Jews from these fortifications; for what could the hands, or military engines of men, avail, against such towers as these?" And he refused to be crowned, after the victory, saying, "That he was not the author of this achievement, but the anger of God against the Jews, was what put the victory into his hands."

3. Finally, the consequences of this catastrophe were as distinctly predicted, and as accurately fulfilled, as the preceding events. The Jews, who survived, were dispersed over the world, in which condition they continue until this day. The Christians, availing themselves of the warnings of their Lord, escaped all the calamities of the siege. Jerusalem was trodden down of the Gentiles; and continues thus to be trodden down, until this day.

Jerusalem was rebuilt by Adrian, but not precisely on the old site; and was called Ælia, which name it bore, until the time of Constantine. The apostate Julian, out of hatred to Christianity, and with the view of defeating the prediction, "That Jerusalem should be trodden down by the Gentiles," determined to restore the Jews, and rebuild their temple. Immense sums were appropriated for the work; the superintendence of which was assigned to one of his lieutenants; and the governor of the province to which Jerusalem belonged, assisted in it. "But horrible balls of fire, bursting forth from the foundations, rendered the place inaccessible to the workmen, who were often much burnt, so that the enterprise was laid aside." The account now given is attested by Julian himself, and his favorite heathen historian, Ammianus. The witnesses are indeed numerous, and unexceptionable; "Annnianus Marcellinus, a heathen; Zemach David, a Jew, who confesses that Julian was, divinitus impeditus, providentially hindered, in his attempt; Nazianzen and Chrysostom, among the Greeks; Ambrose and Ruffin, among the Latins; all of whom flourished, at the very time when this wonderful event occurred. Theodoret, Socrates, Sozomen, and Philostorgius, respectable historians, recorded it within fifty years after the event; and while the eye witnesses of the fact were still surviving." [30] That part of the prophecy, which relates to the restoration of the Jews, remains to be accomplished, and we hope the accomplishment is not far distant. When this event shall take place, the evidence from this prophecy will be complete, and almost irresistible. This shall occur when "The times of the Gentiles shall be fulfilled." The circumstances of this glorious event, are more particularly described by Paul, in his Epistle to the Romans, chap. xi. "If the fall if them be the riches. of the world, and the diminishing of them the riches of the Gentiles; how much more their fulness? for I would not, brethren, that ye should be ignorant of this mystery, that blindness in part is happened to Israel, until the fulness of the Gentiles be come in; and so all Israel shall be saved." The preaching of the Gospel to all nations, has been considered in another place.

After this concise review of some remarkable prophecies contained in the Bible, is there any one, who can persuade himself, that all these coincidences are accidental? or that the whole is a cunningly, devised fable? That man must indeed be blind, who cannot see "This Light which shineth in a dark place:"--"This SURE WORD OF PROPHECY, which holy men of God spake as they were moved by the Holy Ghost."

*Archibald Alexander, D. D.*

## *Footnotes:*
19. Jer. x. 15.
20. Lam. iv. 19.
21. 2 Kings, xviii. 9, 10.
22. 2 Kings, xxv. 10.
23. 2 Kings, vi. 5.
24. 2 Kings, xxv. 3.
25. Josephus de Jud. Bello.
26. Jer. xxvi. 29; Deut. xxviii. 53.
27. 2 Kings, vi. 28, 29.
28. Lam. iv. 10.
29. Isa. xliv. xlv.
30. See Whitby's General Preface to the New Testament.

## CHAPTER IX – NO OTHER RELIGION POSSESSES THE SAME KIND AND DEGREE OF EVIDENCE AS CHRISTIANITY: AND NO OTHER MIRACLES ARE AS WELL ATTESTED, AS THOSE RECORDED IN THE BIBLE

HAVING given a brief view of the external evidences of Christianity, it is now proper to inquire, whether any system of religion, ancient or modern, is as well supported by evidence; and whether, other miracles have testimony in their favor, as satisfactory, as that by which the miracles of the Gospel are accompanied.

The usual declamation of infidel writers, on this subject, is calculated to make the impression on unsuspicious readers, that all religions are similar in their origin;--that they all lay claim to miracles and divine communications;--and that all stand upon an equal footing. But when we descend to particulars, and inquire, what religions that now exist, or ever did exist, profess to rest their claims on well attested miracles, and the exact accomplishment, of prophecy, none besides the Jewish and Christian can be produced. Among the multiform systems of Paganism, there is not one, which was founded on manifest miracles or prophecies. They had, indeed, their prodigies and their oracles, by which the credulous multitude were deceived; and their founders pretended to have received revelations, or to have held communion with the gods. But what well attested miraculous fact can be produced, from all the religions of the heathen world? What oracle ever gave responses so clear and free from ambiguity, as to furnish evidence, that the knowledge of futurity was possessed? It is easy to pretend to divine revelation: this is done by every fanatic.

It is not disputed, that many impostors have appeared in the world, as well as many deluded fanatics. But the reason why all their claims and pretensions may with propriety be rejected, is, that they were not able to exhibit any satisfactory evidence, that they were commissioned from heaven, to instruct mankind in religion.

In this we are all agreed. Of what use, therefore, can it be, to bring up these impostures and delusions, when the evidences of the Christian religion are under consideration? Can it be a reason for rejecting a religion which comes well attested, that there have been innumerable false pretensions to divine revelation? Must miracles, supported by abundant testimony, be discredited, because there have been reports of prodigies and miracles which have no evidence? And because heathen oracles have given answers to inquiries respecting future events, dark, indeterminate, and designedly ambiguous; shall we place no confidence in numerous authentic prophecies, long ago committed to writing, which have been most exactly and wonderfully accomplished?

It is alleged, that the early history of all ancient nations is fabulous, and abounds in stories of incredible prodigies; and hence it is inferred, that the miracles of the Old and New Testament, should be considered in the same light. To which it may be replied, that this general consent of nations, that miracles have existed, is favorable to the opinion that true miracles have at some time occurred. It may again be observed, that the history of Moses, which is more than a thousand years older than any profane history, has every deuce of being a true relation of facts;--and, moreover, that the age in which the miracles of the New Testament were performed, so far from being a dark and fabulous age, was the most enlightened period of the heathen world. It was the age of the most celebrated historians, orators, and poets. There never was a time, when it would have been more difficult to gain a general belief in miracles, which had no sufficient testimony, than in the Augustan, and succeeding age. Not only did learning flourish; but there was at that period, a general tendency to skepticism and atheism. There can evidently, therefore, be no inference unfavorable to Christianity, derived from the belief of unfounded stories of miraculous events, in the dark ages of antiquity. The only effect of the prevalence of false accounts of miracles, should be, to produce caution and careful examination into the evidence of every report of this kind. Reason dictates, that truth and falsehood should never be confounded. Let every fact

*Archibald Alexander, D. D.*

be subjected to the test of a rigid scrutiny, and let it stand or fall, according as it. is supported or unsupported by testimony. If the miracles of the Bible have no better evidence than the prodigies of the heathen, they ought to receive no more credit; but if they have solid evidence, they ought not to be confounded with reports which carry imposture on their very face; or, at least, have no credible testimony in their favor.

There is no other way of deciding on facts, which occurred long since, but by testimony. And the truth of Christianity is really a matter of fact. In support of it, we have adduced testimony which cannot be invalidated; and we challenge our opponents to show, that any other religion stands on the same firm basis. Instead of this, they would amuse us with vague declamations on the credulity of man, and the many fabulous stories which have been circulated and believed. But what has this to do with the question? We admit all this, and maintain that it does not furnish the semblance of an argument against the truth of the well attested facts, recorded by the evangelists. Because there is much falsehood in the world, is there no such thing as. truth? It would be just as reasonable to conclude, that, because many men have been convicted of false, hood, there were no persons of veracity in the world; or that because there were many knaves, all pretensions, to honesty were unfounded.

The Mohammedan religion is frequently brought forward by the enemies of revelation, with an air of confidence, as though the pretensions and success of that impostor, would derogate from the evidences of Christianity. It is expedient, therefore, to bring this, subject under a particular examination. And here, let it be observed, that we do not reject any timing, respecting the origin and progress of this religion, which has been transmitted to us by competent and credible witnesses. We admit that Mohammed existed, and was the founder of a new sect; and, that from a small be, ginning, his religion spread with astonishing rapidity over the fairest portion of the globe. We admit, also, that he was the author of the Koran, which he composed, from time to time, probably with the aid of some one or two, other persons. Moreover, it is admitted;, that he was an extraordinary man, and prosecuted the. bold scheme which he had projected, with uncommon perseverance and address. Neither are we disposed to deny, that the Koran contains many sublime passages, relative to God and his perfections, and many sound and salutary precepts of morality. That the language is elegant, and a standard of purity in the Arabic tongue, has been asserted by all Mohammedan writers, and conceded by many learned Christians. But as to his pretended revelations, there is no external evidence, whatever, that they were real; and there is an overwhelming weight of internal evidence, that they are not from God.

To bring this subject fairly before us, let the following considerations be impartially weighed:

1. The pretensions of Mohammed were supported by no miracles, or prophecies. Ile was often called upon by his opposers to confirm his mission, by this decisive proof; but he always declined making the attempt; and resorted to various excuses and subterfuges. In the Koran, God is introduced, as saying, "Nothing hindered us from sending thee with miracles, except that the former nations have charged them with imposture:--thou art a preacher only." Again, "That if he did perform miracles, the people would not believe, as they had before rejected Moses, Jesus, and the prophets, who performed them."

Dr. Paley [31] has enumerated thirteen different places in the Koran, where this objection is considered, in not one of which, it is alleged, that miracles had been performed for its confirmation. It is true, that this artful man told of things, sufficiently miraculous; but for the truth of these assertions, we have no manner of proof, except his own word, which, in this case, is worth nothing.

Now, if it had been as easy a thing to obtain credit to stories of miracles, publicly performed, as some suppose, surely Mohammed would have had recourse to this measure, during the period, that he was so pressed and teased by his enemies, with a demand for this very evidence. But he had too much cunning to venture upon an expedient so dangerous: his opposers Would quickly have detected and exposed the cheat. At length, however, he so far yielded to the demand of his enemies, as to publish one of the most extravagant stories, which ever entered into the imagination of man; and solemnly swore that every word of it was true. I refer to his night journey to Jerusalem, and thence to heaven, under the guidance of the angel Gabriel. As this story may afford some amusement to the reader, I will subjoin, in a note, the substance of it, omitting those particulars which are most ridiculous and extravagant. [32]

This marvellous story, however, had well nigh ruined his cause. His enemies treated it with deserved ridicule and scorn; and a number of his followers forsook him, from that time. In fact, it rendered his further continuance at Mecca, entirely inexpedient; and having before despatched some of his disciples to Medina, he betook himself, with his followers, to that city, where he met with a more cordial reception, than in his native place.

The followers of Mohammed, hundreds of years after his death, related many miracles, which they pretended that he performed: but their report is not only unsupported by testimony, but is in direct contradiction to the Koran, where he repeatedly disclaims all pretensions to miraculous powers. And the miracles which they ascribe to him, while they are marvellous enough, are of that trifling and ludicrous kind, commonly to be met with in all forgeries, in which miracles are represented as having been performed; such as, that the trees walked to meet him;--that the stones saluted him;--that a beam groaned to him;--that a camel made complaint to him;--and that a shoulder of mutton told him that it was poisoned.

It appears, then, that Mohammedanism has no evidence, whatever, but the declaration of the impostor. It is impossible, therefore, that. Christianity should be placed in a more favorable point of light, than in comparison with the religion of Mohammed. The one, as we have seen, rests on well attested miracles; the other does not exhibit the shadow of a proof, that it was derived from heaven.

2. It is fair to compare the moral characters of the respective founders of these two religions. And here we have as perfect a contrast as history can furnish. Jesus Christ was, holy, harmless, undefiled, and separate from sinners. His life was pure, without a stain. His most bitter enemies could find no fault in him. He exhibited, through life, the most perfect example of disinterested zeal, pure benevolence, and unaffected humility, which the world ever saw. Mohammed was an ambitious, licentious, cruel, and unjust man. His life was stained with the most atrocious crimes. Blasphemy, perjury, murder, adultery, lust, and robbery, were actions of daily occurrence. And to shield himself from censure, and open a door for unbridled indulgence, he pretended revelations from heaven, to justify all his vilest practices. He had the effrontery to pretend, that God had given him privilege to commit, at pleasure, the most abominable crimes. The facts which could be adduced in support of these general charges, are so numerous, and so shocking, that I will not defile my paper, nor wound the feelings of the reader, by a recital of them.

3. The Koran itself can never bear a comparison with the New Testament, in the view of any impartial person. It is a confused and incongruous heap of sublime sentiments, moral precepts, positive institutions, extravagant and ridiculous stories, and manifest lies and contradictions. Mohammed, himself, acknowledged, that it contained many contradictions; but he accounted for this fact by alleging, that what had been communicated to him in one chapter, was repealed in a subsequent one;--and so he charges this inconsistency on his Maker. The number of abrogated passages is so great, that a mussulman cannot be easily confuted by proving the falsehood of any declaration in the Koran; for, he will have recourse to this doctrine of abrogation. There is nothing in this book, which cannot easily be accounted for; nothing above the capacity of impostors to accomplish. It is artfully accommodated to the religions of Arabia, prevalent at the time. It gives encouragement to the strongest and most vicious passions of human nature; promotes ambition, despotism, revenge, and offensive war; opens wide the door of licentiousness; and holds out such rewards and punishments, as are calculated to make an impression on the minds of wicked men. It discourages, and indeed forbids, all free inquiry, and all discussion of the doctrines which it contains. Whatever is excellent in the Koran, is in imitation of the Bible; but wherever the author follows his own judgment, or indulges his own imagination, we find falsehood, impiety, or ridiculous absurdity. [33]

4. The means by which the religion of Mohammed was propagated, were entirely different from those employed in the propagation of the Gospel. If there is any point of strong resemblance between these two systems, it consists merely in the circumstance of the rapid and extensive progress, and permanent continuance, of each. But when we come to consider the means by which this end was attained in the two cases, instead of resemblance we find again, a perfect contrast. Mohammed did, indeed, attempt, at first, to propagate his religion by persuasion and artifice; and these efforts he continued for twelve years, but with very small success. At the end of three years, he had gained no more than fourteen disciples; and at. the end of seven years, his followers amounted to little more than eighty; and at the end of twelve years, when he fled from Mecca, the number was very inconsiderable. As far, therefore, as there can be a fair comparison between the progress of Christianity and Mohammedanism; that is, during the time that Mohammed employed argument and persuasion alone, there is no resemblance. The progress of Christianity was like the lightning, which shineth from one part of heaven to the other; extending in a few years, not only without aid from learning and power, but in direct opposition to both, throughout the whole Roman empire, and far beyond its limits. But Mohammedanism, for twelve years, made scarcely any progress; yet it commenced among an ignorant and uncivilized people. During this period, the progress was scarcely equal to what might be expected from any artful impostor. This religion never spread in any other way than by the sword. As soon as the inhabitants of Medina declared in favor of Mohammed, he changed his whole plan, and gave out that he was directed to propagate his religion by force. From this time, he is found engaged in war. He began by attacking mercantile caravans, and, as his force increased, went on to conquer the petty kingdoms, into which Arabia was then divided. [34] Sometimes, he put all the prisoners to death, and at other times, sold them into slavery. At first, the order was, to massacre. every creature that refused to embrace his religion; but he became more lenient afterwards, especially to Jews and Christians. The alternative was, "The Koran, death, or tribute."

But it is a great mistake, to suppose, that the conquests of Mohammed, himself, were very extensive. The fact is, that he, never, during his life, extended his dominion. beyond the limits of Arabia; except, that he overran one or two inconsiderable provinces of Syria. It was by the Caliphs, his successors, that so great a part of Asia, and Egypt, were brought into subjection. But what is there remarkable in these successes, more than those of other conquerors? Surely, the propagation of

Mohammedanism by the sword, however rapid or extensive, can never bear any comparison with that of Christianity, by the mere force of truth, under the blessing of heaven.

5. The tendency and effects of Mohammedanism, when compared with the tendency and effects of Christianity, serve to exhibit the latter in a very favorable light. The Christian religion has been a rich blessing to every country which has embraced it; and its salutary effects have borne proportion to the care which has been taken to inculcate its genuine principles, and the cordiality with which its doctrines have been embraced. if we cast our eyes over the map of the world, and inquire what nations are truly civilized? Where does learning flourish? Where are the principles of morality and the dictates of humanity best understood? Where are the poor and afflicted most effectually relieved? Where do men enjoy the greatest security of life, property, and liberty? Where is the female sex treated with due respect, and exalted to their proper place in society? Where is the education of youth most assiduously pursued? Where are the brightest examples of benevolence; and where do men enjoy most rational happiness?--I say, if we were called upon to designate those countries, in which these advantages are, moat highly enjoyed, every one of them would be found in Christendom; and the superiority enjoyed by some over the others, would be found to bear an exact proportion to the practical influence of pure Christianity.

On the contrary, if we take a survey of the rich and salubrious regions, possessed by Mohammedans, we behold a wide spread desolation. The fairest portion of the globe, where arts, literature, and refinement, formerly most flourished, are now blighted. Every noble institution has sunk into oblivion. Despotism extends its iron sceptre over these ill-fated countries, and all the tranquillity ever enjoyed, is the dead calm of ignorance and slavery. Useful learning is discouraged; free inquiry proscribed, and servile submission required of all. Justice is perverted, or disregarded. No man has any security for life or property; and as to liberty, it is utterly lost, wherever the Mohammedan religion prevails. While the fanatic ardor of making proselytes continued, the fury of the propagators of this faith rendered them irresistible. Indeed, their whole system is adapted to a state of war. The best work that can be performed, according to the Koran, is to fight for the propagation of the faith; and the highest rewards are promised to those who die in battle. There is no doubt, but that the principles of the Koran greatly contributed to the conquests of the Saracens; by divesting them of all fear of death, and inspiring them with an assurance of being admitted into a sensual paradise, if it should be their fate to be slain in battle. "The sword," said he, "is the key of heaven and hell: a drop of blood shed in the cause of God, a night spent under arms, is of more avail than two months of fasting and prayer. Whosoever falls in battle, his sins are forgiven. At the day of judgment, his wounds shall be resplendent as vermillion, and odoriferous as musk; and the loss of his limbs shall be replaced by the wings of angels and cherubim." But when they had finished their conquests, and a state of peace succeeded their long and bloody wars, they sunk into torpid indolence and stupidity. While other nations have been making rapid improvements in all the arts, they have remained stationary; or rather have been continually going backward. They have derived no advantages from the revival of letters, the invention of printing, or the improvement in the arts and sciences. The people who have been subjected to their despotism, without adopting their religion, are kept in the most degrading subjection.

At present, [35] the Greeks are making noble exertions to break the cruel yoke, which has oppressed them, and though unsupported by Christian nations, have succeeded in expelling the Turks from a large portion of their country. God grant them success, and give them wisdom to make a good use of their liberty and independence, when acquired and established! [36] Mohammedanism was permitted to prevail, as a just punishment to Christians, for their luxury and dissensions. It is to be hoped, however, that the prescribed time of these locusts of the abyss, [37] is nearly come to an end; and that a just God, who has so long used them as a scourge to Christians, as he formerly did the Canaanites to be thorns in the eyes and in the skies of the Israelites, will soon bring to an end this horrible despotism, which has been founded on a vile imposture. The signs of the times give strong indications, that the Mohammedan power will shortly be subverted. But it is not for us "to know the times and the seasons, which the Father hath put in his own power."

The only thing further, necessary to be considered, in this chapter, is, the miracles which have been brought forward as a counterpoise to the miracles of Christ and his apostles. This is an old stratagem--at. least as early as the second century, when one, Philostratus, at the request of Julia Augusta, wife of the emperor Severus, wrote a history, or rather romance, of Apollonius of Tyana, a town in Capadocia. This Apollonius, was nearly contemporary with Jesus Christ; but whether he was a philosopher, or a conjurer, cannot now be ascertained; for as to the story of Philostratus, which is still extant, it is totally unsupported by any reference to eye-witnesses of the facts, or any documents of credit, and has, throughout, as much the air of extravagant fiction, as any thing that was ever published. That the design of the writer was to set up this Apollonius as a rival to Jesus Christ, is not avowed, but is sufficiently evident from the similarity of many of the miracles ascribed to him, to facts recorded in the Gospels, and which are manifestly borrowed from the evangelical history. He is made to raise the dead, to cast out demons, and to rise from the dead, himself. In one instance, the very words of the demons expelled by Jesus Christ, as recorded by St. Luke, "Art thou come to torment us before the time," are put into the mouth of a demon, said to be cast out by Apollonius. But in addition to these miracles, his biographer pretends, that he saw beasts with a human head and lion's body;--women half white and half black;--together with phoenixes, griffins, dragons, and similar fabulous monsters.

In the fourth century, Hierocles, a bitter enemy of Christianity, instituted a comparison between Jesus and Apollonius, in which, after considering their miracles, he gives the preference to the latter. This book was answered by Eusebius, from whose work only, we can now learn how Hierocles treated the subject, as the book of the latter is not extant. The only conclusion which can be deduced from this history of Apollonius, is, that the miracles of Christ were so firmly believed, in the second century, and were attended by such testimony, that, the enemies of Christianity could not deny the facts, and therefore resorted to the expedient of circulating stories of equal miracles performed by another.

Modern infidels have not been ashamed to resort to the same stale device. Mr. Hume has taken much pains to bring forward a great array of evidence, in favor of certain miracles, in which he has no faith, with the view of discrediting the truth of Christianity. These have been so fully and satisfactorily considered by Dr. Douglass, Bishop of Salisbury, in his Criterion; and Dr. Campbell, in his Essay on Miracles, that I need only refer to these learned authors, for a complete confutation of Hume's arguments, from this source.

For the sake, however, of those who may not have access to these works, I will lay down a few general principles, by which we may distinguish between true and false miracles; for which I am indebted, principally, to the author of the Criterion, above mentioned.

1. The nature of the facts should be well considered, whether they are miraculous. The testimony which supports a fact may be sufficient, and yet it may have been brought about by natural causes.

The miracles of Jesus Christ were such, that there was no room for doubt respecting their supernatural character; but a great part of those performed by others, which have received the best attestation, were of such a nature, that they may readily be accounted for, without supposing any divine interposition. The case of the man diseased in his eyes, said to have been cured by Vespasian's rubbing his hand over them, and the lame man cured by a touch of the emperor's foot, were, no doubt, impositions practised by the priests of the temple, where they were performed. The emperor did not pretend to possess any miraculous power, and was induced, only after much persuasion, to make the experiment. The facts, as related by Tacitus, though he was not an eye-witness--it may be admitted--are true. Such persons were probably brought forward, and a cure pretended to be made, but there is no evidence that there was a real miracle. There was no one present who felt interested, to examine into the truth of the miracle. The priests, who proposed the thing, had, no doubt, prepared their subjects; and the emperor was flattered by the honor of being selected by their god, to work a miracle. How often do beggars in the street impose upon many, by pretending to be blind and lame? The high encomiums which Mr. Flume bestows on the historian Tacitus, in order to set off the testimony to the best advantage, can have. no weight here; for he only related what he bad heard from others, and showed pretty evidently, that. he did not credit the story himself.

The same may be said, respecting the man spoken of by Cardinal de Retz, at Saragossa, who was represented as having been seen without a leg, but obtained one by rubbing the stump with holy oil. The cardinal had no other evidence of his having ever been maimed, than the suspicious report of the canons of the Church; and he took no pains to ascertain, whether the leg which he obtained, was really flesh and blood, or an artificial limb.

A great part of the cures said to have been performed at the tomb of the Abbé Paris, were proved, upon examination, to be mere pretences; and those, which were real, may easily be accounted for, from the influence of a heated imagination, and enthusiastic feelings; especially, since we have seen the wonderful effects of animal magnetism, and metallic tractors. [38]

2. A second consideration of great weight, is, that in true miracles, we can trace the testimony to the very time time when the facts are said to have occurred, but in false miracles, the report of the facts originates a long time afterwards, as in the case of Apollonius. And in the case of the miracles ascribed to Mohammed by Abulfeda and Al-Janabbi; and, also, of the miracles ascribed by the Jesuits, to Ignatius Loyola, their founder; which were never heard of, until long after his death.

3. Another criterion of importance, is, that the report of miracles should originate, and first obtain credit, in the place, and among the people, where they are said to have been performed. This is too remarkably the fact, in regard to the miracles of the Bible, to require any proof. But many stories of miracles are rendered suspicious by the circumstance that they were first reported and believed, in some place, far from that in which they were alleged to have been wrought. The miracles ascribed by the Romanists to Francis Xavier, are condemned by both the rules last mentioned. In all his letters, while a missionary in the east, he never hints that miracles had been wrought; and a reputable writer, who gave some account of his labors, nearly forty years after his death, not only is silent about Xavier's miracles, but confesses, that no miracles had been performed among the Indians. These miracles were said to be performed in the remote parts of India, and Japan, but the report of them was published first, in Europe.

Almost all the miracles ascribed by the Romish Church, to her saints, fall into the same predicament. The history of them was written long after they are said to have been performed, and often in countries remote from the place where it is pretended they occurred.

4. Another thing necessary to be taken into view, in judging of the genuineness of miracles, is, whether the facts were scrutinized at the time, or were suffered to pass without examination. When the miracles reported, coincide with the passions and prejudices of those before whom they are performed;--when they are exhibited by persons in power, who can prevent all examination, and put what face they please on facts, they may well be reckoned suspicious. Now, the cures at the tomb of the Abbé Paris, were not performed in these circumstances. The Jansenists were not in power, and their enemies not only had the opportunity to examine into the facts, but actually did so, with the utmost diligence. We have reason to believe, therefore, that we have now a true report of those occurrences. The defect of these miracles is, in their nature, not in their evidence.

But in most cases, the miracles which have been reported, took place, when there was no opportunity of examining into the facts--when the people were pleased to be confirmed in their favorite opinions--or, when the ruling powers had some particular end to answer. [39]

But, supposing these miracles to be ever so well attested, I do not perceive how the evidence of divine revelation can be affected by them; for, if it could be made to appear, that these were supported by testimony, as strong as that which can be adduced in favor of the miracles of the New Testament, the only fair conclusion is, that, in consistency, they who believe in Christianity, should admit them to be true--but what then? Would it follow, because miracles had been wrought on some rare occasions, different from those recorded in the Bible, that, therefore, these were of no validity, as evidence of divine revelation? Would not the fact, that other miracles had been wrought, rather confirm our belief in those which were performed with so important a design? Mr. Hume does, indeed, artfully insinuate, that the various accounts of miracles which exist, cannot be true, because the religions which they were wrought to confirm, are opposite; yet not one of those which he brings forward, as being best attested, was performed in confirmation of any new religion, or to prove any particular doctrine, therefore they are not opposed to Christianity. If they had actually occurred, it would not in the least disparage the evidence for the facts recorded in the New Testament. And, especially, it is a strange conceit, that miracles performed within the bosom of the Christian Church, should furnish any proof against Christianity.

It is, however, no part of the object of those who bring forward such an array of testimony, in support of certain miracles, to prove that such facts ever occurred. This is diametrically opposite to their purpose. Their design is, to discredit all testimony in favor of miracles, by showing, that facts acknowledged to be false, have evidence as strong as those ou which revealed religion rests. But they have utterly failed in the attempt, as we have shown; and if they had succeeded in adducing as strong testimony for other miracles, then we would readily admit their truth, and that, in perfect consistency with our belief in Christianity.

## *Footnotes:*

31. Paley's Evidences.
32. See Note A.
33. See Ryan's History of the Effects of Religion on Mankind.
34. See Prideaux's Life of Mahomet.
35. A. D. 1825
36. Since the above was written, several of the governments of Europe have interposed to rescue the Greeks from the persecution and oppression of the Ottoman power; but they are yet in a very unsettled state, and it cannot be foreseen what will be the result of all their struggles. A. D. 1832.
37. Rev. ix. 3.
38. See Note B.
39. On this whole subject, see Douglass' Criterion.

# CHAPTER X - THE BIBLE CONTAINS INTERNAL EVIDENCE THAT ITS ORIGIN IS DIVINE

As the Old and New Testaments are intimately connected, and form parts of the same system, it is unnecessary to make any distinction between them, in considering this branch of the evidence of divine revelation.

A late writer, [40] of great eminence and popularity, has represented this species of evidence as unsatisfactory; as not capable of being so treated, as to produce conviction in the minds of philosophical infidels; and as opening a door to their most specious objections to Christianity. But, certainly, this is not the most effectual method of supporting the credit of the Scriptures. Another popular writer [41] has gone to the other extreme; and seems to set little value on the external evidences of Christianity, while be exhibits the internal, in a light so strong, that his argument assumes the appearance of demonstration.

But these two species of evidence, though distinct, are harmonious, and strengthen each other. There is, therefore, no propriety in disparaging the one, for the purpose of enhancing the value of the other. I believe, the fact is, however, that more instances have occurred of skeptical men being convinced of the truth of Christianity, by the internal, than the external evidences. It is the misfortune of most infidels, that they have no intimate acquaintance with the Bible; and even many of those who have undertaken to write against it, appear never to have read it, with any other view, than to find some ground of objection.

No doubt, it is necessary to come to the examination of this species of evidence, with a candid and docile disposition. If reason be permitted proudly to assume the seat of judgment, and to undertake to decide what a revelation ought to contain in particular; in what manner, and with what degree of light it should be communicated; whether it should be made perfectly at once, or gradually unfolded; and whether, from the beginning, it should be universal: no doubt, the result of an examination of the contents of the Bible, conducted on such principles, will prove unsatisfactory; and insuperable objections will occur .at every step in the progress. It was wise in Dr. Chalmers, to endeavor to discourage such a mode of investigation, as being most unreasonable; for how is it possible, that such a creature as man, should be able to know what is proper for the infinite God to do, or in what way he should deal with his creatures upon earth? To borrow the language of this powerful writer; [42] "We have experience of man, but we have no experience of God. We can reason Upon the procedure of man in given circumstances, because this is an accessible subject, and comes under the cognizance of observation; but we cannot reason on the procedure of the Almighty in given circumstances." But when he speaks "of disclaiming all support from what is commonly understood by the internal evidence," and "saving a vast deal of controversy, by proving that all this is superfluous and uncalled for," I am constrained to think, that, instead of aiding the cause of Christianity, the excellent author has attempted to take away one of its firmest props. The internal evidence of revelation is analogous to the evidence of the being and perfections of God, from the works of creation: and the same mode of reasoning winch the deist adopts, relative to the doctrines and institutions of the Bible, the atheist may adopt, with equal force, against the existence of a God. If men will be so presumptuous as to determine, that if God makes a world, he will form it according to their idea of fitness, and that the apparent imperfections and incomprehensibilities in the material universe, could never have proceeded from a Being of infinite perfection, atheism must follow of course. But, if, notwithstanding all these apparent evils and obscurities, there is in the structure of the world, the most convincing evidence of the existence of an all-wise and all-powerful Being; why may we not expect to find the same kind of evidence, impressed on a revelation from God? Upon Dr. Chalmers' principles, we ought to depend simply on historical testimony, for the fact, that God created this world; and "disclaim all support" from what. may, without, impropriety, be termed the internal evidence of the existence of God, derived from the contemplation of the work itself. The truth, however, is, that every thing which proceeds from God, whatever difficulties or obscurities accompany it, will contain and exhibit the impress of his character. As this is resplendently visible in the heavens and the earth, it is reasonable to. think that it will not be less manifest in his word. If the truths contained in a revelation be worthy of God, they will be stamped with his image; and if this can be, in any measure, discovered, undoubtedy it furnishes the most direct and convincing evidence of their divine origin. In fact this is, without being reduced to the form of a regular argument, precisely the evidence on which the faith of the great body of Christians has always rested. They are incapable of appreciating the force of the external evidence. It requires an extent, of learning, which plain laboring Christians, cannot be supposed commonly to posse.. But the internal evidence is within their reach: it acts directly upon their minds, whenever they read or hear a portion of the word of God. The belief of common, unlearned Christians, is not necessarily founded in the mere prejudice of education: it rests on the best possible evidence. And as there is a faith which is saving, and to which a purifying efficacy is ascribed; if we inquire, on what species of evidence this depends, it must be answered, on internal evidence: not, indeed, as perceived by the unaided intellect of man, but as it is. exhibited to the mind, by the illumination of the Holy Spirit. We cannot consent, therefore, to give up this species of evidence, as "superfluous and uncalled for," but must consider it, if not the most effectual to silence gainsayers, yet certainly the most useful to the real Christian; and if unbelievers could be induced to attend to it, with docility and impartiality, there is reason to think, that they would experience its efficacy, in the gradual production of a firm conviction of the truth of Christianity. The internal evidence of the truth of the Scriptures, cannot be fully brought into view, in any other way, than by a careful study of the Bible. It cannot easily be put into the form, of logical argument, for it consists in moral fitness and beauty: in the adaptation of truth to the constitution of the human mind; in its astonishing power of penetrating and searching the heart, and affecting the conscience. There is a sublime sanctity in the doctrines and precepts of the Gospel; a devotional and heavenly spirit pervading the Scriptures; a purity and holy tendency, which cannot but be felt by the serious reader of the word of God; and a power to soothe and comfort the sorrowful mind: all which qualities may be perceived, and will have their effect, but cannot be embodied and presented, with their full force, in the form of argument. But, although this evidence, from the nature of the case, cannot be exhibited in its entire body, to any but those who study the Scriptures, and meditate on their truths, day and night, yet it is possible to select some prominent points, and present them to the reader, in such a light., as to produce a salutary impression. This is what will now be briefly attempted, in the following remarks, which might, without difficulty, be greatly enlarged:

1. The Scriptures speak of God and his attributes; in a way which accords with what right reason would lead us to expect, in a divine revelation. He is uniformly represented in the Bible, as ONE, and as a Being of infinite perfection; as eternal,--omnipotent,--omniscient,--omnipresent--and immutable. And it is truly remarkable, that these correct and sublime views of theology were entertained by those who possessed the Scriptures, when all other nations had fallen into the grossest polytheism, and most degrading idolatry. Other nations were more powerful, and greatly excelled the Israelites in human learning; but in the knowledge of God, all were in thick darkness, whilst this people enjoyed the light of truth. Learned men and philosophers arose in different countries, and obtained celebrity on account of their theories, but they effected no change in the popular opinions; indeed, they could not enlighten others, when they were destitute of the light of truth, themselves. However deists may deride and scoff at the Bible, it is a fact capable of the clearest proof, that had it not been for the Scriptures, there would, not, at this time, be such a thing as pure theist upon earth. There is not now in the world, an individual who believes in one infinitely perfect God, whose knowledge of this truth may not be traced, directly or indirectly, to the Bible.

How can it be accounted for, that the true theology should be found accompanying the Scriptures, in ages, while it was last, every where else, unless we admit that they are a revelation from God? If the knowledge of the true God, as received by the Jews, was the discovery of reason, why was it that other nations, advanced far beyond them in learning and mental culture, never arrived at the knowledge of his important truth?

It is true, indeed, that the Scriptures sometimes represent God as having bodily parts, and human passions; but a little consideration will show the attentive reader that all these expressions are used in accommodation to the manner of speaking among men. The truth is, that all human language is inadequate to express the attributes and operations of the Supreme Being. He is infinitely above our conceptions,. both in his essence; and mode of existence and acting. We can do no more than approximate towards just ideas, on this subject. When we speak of Him, we are under the necessity of conceiving of his perfections, with some relation to the operations of the human mind, and to employ language expressive of human acts, and feelings: for all other language would be unintelligible. The necessity of this accomodation extends much thriller than many seem to suppose: it exists not only in relation to words, which taken literally, convey the idea of bodily members and human passions, but also in regard to those which express the operations of will and intellect. This mode of speaking, therefore, instead of-being an objection against the Bible, is an argument of the wisdom of its Author, who has spoken to man in the only way in which he could be understood.

Again, it is seen by the most cursory reader, that truth is not taught in the Bible, in a scientific, or-systematic order. We have here no profound metaphysical disquisitions; no discussion of philosophical principles; no array of artificial dialectics; and no systematic arrangement of the subjects treated. In all this, there may be great wisdom, and whether we. can see the reason or not, the objection to revelation,

*The Evidences of the Christian Religion*

on this ground, is not greater than the one which may be made to the natural world, because the materials for building, which it contains, are not found erected into houses; and because all its fields and forests, are not placed in the order of an artificial garden, or regular orchard.

The method of speaking of God, in the Sacred Scriptures, is at once most simple, and sublime. Few words are employed, but these are most significant., When Moses wished to receive an appropriate name, which he might mention to Pharaoh, to whom he was sent, he was directed to say, I am that I am hath sent me. And when, on another occasion, the name of the Most High was declared to Moses, it was in the following remarkable words, THE LORD, THE LORD GOD, MERCIFUL AND GRACIOUS, LONG SUFFERING AND ABUNDANT IN GOODNESS AND TRUTH. KEEPING MERCY FOR THOUSANDS; FORGIVING INIQUITY, AND TRANSGRESSION AND SIN; AND THAT WILL BY NO MEANS CLEAR THE GUILTY. If the most perfect simplicity, united with the highest sublimity, would be received as a proof; that the writers of these books were inspired, we could adduce hundreds of passages of this description; but we mean not to lay any undue stress on the argument derived from this source.

The glory of the Scriptures is, the revelation which they contain of the moral attributes of God. These are manifested with but a feeble light, in the works of creation; but, in the Bible they shine with transcendent lustre. It would, by no means comport with the intended brevity of this work, to enter much into detail on this subject, but I must beg the indulgence of the reader, while I endeavor to bring distinctly into view, the account which the Scriptures give us, of the HOLINESS, and the GOODNESS of GOD.

These two attributes are stamped on the pages of the Bible, and form its grand characteristic. It is of no importance, whether we consider these as distinct, or as expressive of two aspects, in which the same infinite excellence is exhibited. Who can open this sacred book, without perceiving that the God of the Bible was Holy? All his laws, institutions, and dispensations, are holy; even those laws which are ceremonial, have this characteristic. Every person, edifice, and utensil, employed in his worship, must be solemnly consecrated; and all must approach God with caution and reverence, because he is Holy. The very ground where he occasionally makes himself known, is rendered holy. Every external sign and emblem of profound reverence, is required in them, who worship Him; and when he manifests himself with more than usual clearness, the holiest men are overwhelmed, and become as dead men, under a sense of their own vileness. And not only so, but even the heavenly hosts, who are free from every stain of sin, seem to be overwhelmed with the view of the HOLINESS of God: They not only cry to one another, as they worship around his august throne, HOLY, HOLY, HOLY, but they are represented, as falling prostrate at his feet, and veiling their faces, in token of profound veneration. All those passages of Scripture, which speak of the WRATH, the INDIGNATION, the FURY, the JEALOUSY, or the ANGER of the Almighty, are no more than strong expressions of his infinite holiness. All his severe judgments and threatenings; all the misery which he ever inflicts on his creatures, in this world, or the next; and above all, the intense and ineffable sufferings of Christ, are exhibitions of the holiness of God.

Now, if there be a God, he must be holy; and if he make a revelation of himself, it will be marked with. this impress of character. But. wicked men would, never have made this attribute so prominent; they would rather have been disposed to keep it entirely out of view. There is no truth more evident to the attentive observer of human nature, than that men do not naturally love holiness, although they are obliged to acknowledge its worth. This, I believe, is the true reason, why the Scriptures, although they contain the highest excellence in composition, both in prose and poetry, of which a good taste cannot be insensible, are neglected by literary men; or rather studiously avoided. A mere fragment of any other book, if it could claim pp'equal antiquity with. the Bible; and, especially, if it contained any thing like as much excellence of composition, would be sought after with avidity, by all men of taste; but the Bible remains almost as much unstudied by men of this description, as the Koran. This has often appeared to me paradoxical; but I am now persuaded, that the true reason is, the awful holiness of God, as exhibited in this book, and impressed on almost every page. This glares upon the conscience of an unholy man, as the meridian sun on diseased eyes. God is a consuming fire. But this common dislike of the Bible, even in men of refined taste and decent lives, furnishes a strong argument for its divine origin. The question before us, is, who composed this book--inspired men, or wicked impostors? The characteristic, which we have been considering, will accord perfectly with the former supposition, but never can be reconciled with the latter. There is a moral certainty, that base impostors never would have written a book, the most remarkable trait of which is HOLINESS.

The goodness of God, or that benevolence which he exercises towards his creatures, as it appears in the providence which sustains and feeds so great a multitude of creatures, and which is conspicuously manifested to the human family, is often celebrated in the Scriptures. Some of the most beautiful and sublime poems which were ever written, are employed in celebrating the praise of God, for his marvellous goodness. The reader is requested to turn to the xxxiv, the ciii, civ, cxlv, cxlvi, cxlvii, and cxlviii, Psalms, as an exemplification of this remark.

But there is another, and a peculiar view of the divine goodness, given in the Scriptures. It is that form of goodness, called MERCY. It is the love of creatures, who had forfeited all claim to any kindness. It is the bestowing of pardon and salvation on those, who are condemned to death by the righteous laws of God; and this, without showing himself less displeased with their sins, than if he had punished them forever. This is the view of divine goodness, which is peculiar to the Bible. Reason could not have formed a conjecture concerning it. It is the development of a trait in the divine character, before unknown. To reveal the mercy of God, may, with truth, be said, to be the principal object of the Bible. But our idea of this divine goodness is very imperfect, until we learn, in what way it was manifested. No words can express this so well, as those of Christ himself, "God so loved the world, that he gave his only begotten Son, that whosoever believeth on him should not perish, but have everlasting life."

To many, perhaps, it will appear, that this love is so extraordinary, that it rather forms an objection against the Bible, than an argument in its favor. If the wonderful and unparalleled nature of any thing were an objection to it, then I acknowledge, that there would be some ground for this opinion. But what is there which is not full of wonders, when we come to contemplate it attentively? It is wonderful that there should exist such a creature as man, or such a body of light as the sun; but shall we, therefore; refuse to believe in their existence? To conic nearer to the subject, what is there in the character of God, or his works, which is not calculated to fill the mind with surpassing wonder! His eternity--His omniscience--His omnipresence--His creating power, and universal providence, are so wonderful, that we are at a loss to say which is most wonderful; or whether any thing else can be more wonderful. But is this any argument against their reality? And if God is so wonderful in his other attributes, shall we expect to find nothing of this kind, in his LOVE, which is his highest glory? There is, indeed, no goodness of this sort among men; but shall we make our faint and limited shadow of perfection, the measure by which to judge of the character of the infinite God? How unreasonable such a procedure! The objection derived from the insignificance of man, the object of this wonderful love, is delusive; for the same objection would lie, if his powers were increased ever so much. in comparison with God, all creatures may be considered as on a level; in this view, all distinctions among them are, as it were, annihilated. How easy would it be to construct an argument against the providence of God, on the same principles! There are innumerable myriads of animalcules, invisible to man, all of which have a perfect organization, and no more than an ephemeral existence, It might be said, these minute creatures are too diminutive, to occupy the attention of an infinite Being. It might be said, that the display of so much skill in the organization of creatures of a day, was unsuitable to the wisdom of God. But however plausible such objections may be made to appear, they are all founded in a presumptuous intrusion into what does not appertain to us, and concerning which we have no ability to form any correct judgment. The truth is, that man has an infinitude below him, as well as above him, in the gradation of being. I do not mean to say, that creation is absolutely infinite, but that we can fix no bounds to the possibility of a continual existence of creatures in the scale of perpetual diminution, any more than we can to the possibility of creatures still increasing in magnitude above us. In this respect, as in others, we stand between two infinitudes, the great and the small, if I may so speak. A single drop of liquid contains myriads of perfectly organized creatures; and who knows but every particle of the blood of these invisible animalcules may contain other worlds of beings still more minute, without it being possible for us to fix any limit to the diminution in the size of creatures.

But, to return; unless it can be shown, that such love, as that exhibited in the Gospel, is impossible, which will not be pretended, or that it is repugnant to the moral attributes of God, its wonderful nature can never be properly used as an argument against its existence. Rather, it should be argued, the more wonderful, the more like God; the more wonderful, if no appearance of human weakness accompany it, the more unlikely to be the invention of man.

And, here, I would mention an idea, which, if correct, will shed light on the subject; namely, that wonder is congenial to the constitution of our minds. The soul of man never enjoys more elevated emotions, and more exalted pleasure, than in the contemplation of objects so great and vast, as to he perfectly incomprehensible. This is the foundation of that perpetual adoration which occupies the inhabitants of heaven. An incomprehensible God, is the object of contemplation and wonder to every creature.

2. The account which the Bible gives of the origin and character of man, accords, very exactly, with reason and experience.

Indeed, this is the only source of our knowledge respecting the circumstances in which man was placed, when he came from the hand of his Creator. Here we learn the origin of many things which we observe, but the reason of which we never could have discovered. The Bible teaches us, that the wickedness which has existed in all ages and among all people, originated in the apostacy of the first pair. It tells us the reason of covering the body with clothing, which is the custom of all nations, even where clothing is unnecessary to preserve the body from the effects of cold. Here, we learn the cause of the earth's producing briers and thorns spontaneously, while useful grain and fruits must be cultivated. Here, we learn the origin of marriage, and, of the curse which has followed the female sex, through all ages. Moses has also given us the origin of that species of religious worship, which was anciently practised among all people, but of which, reason can teach us nothing. I mean the sacrifice of animals on an altar, and the offerings of grain, of incense, &c. He has also related the fact of a universal deluge, of which we have so many ocular proofs, in every country, and on every mountain, as well as so many ancient traditions.

The dispersion of the human family over the face of the earth, and the origin of the several nations of antiquity, are recorded in the Bible: and, although, this record is contained in a single short chapter, and has to us much obscurity, yet Bishop Watson declared, that if he had no other evidence of the authenticity of the Pentateuch, besides the tenth chapter of Genesis, he would deem that alone satisfactory. [43]

The origin of the diversity of language, is also found in the Bible, and not learned from any other source. Indeed, the origin of language itself, concerning which philosophers have disputed so much, is very evident., from the history of Moses. Many learned men have thought, that alphabetical writing took its rise from the writing of the decalogue, by the finger of God, upon the tables of stone; and I believe, that it would be found very difficult to prove, by any authentic documents, that this art existed before. Be this as it may, it must be admitted, that the earliest specimen of alphabetical writing now extant, is contained in the Bible.

To these particulars it may be added, that we have an account in the Bible, of those nations and people, concerning whom the earliest profane historians treat, long before their histories commence; and when history comes down to that period when the affairs of nations are described by others, it receives ample corroboration from their narratives, as well as gives great light, to enable us to understand many things which they have imperfectly recorded.

But the account which the Bible gives of the moral condition of man, is that which is now most to our purpose. In all ages and circumstances, the human race are represented as exceedingly depraved and wicked. Every man is declared to be a transgressor, and the root of this depravity is placed in the heart. Many of the gross crimes, to which we all are inclined, and into the practice of which many fall, are enumerated; and where these are avoided and concealed, the heart is described as deceitful and desperately wicked; and that pride and hypocrisy, which spread a false covering over the true character of man, are denounced, as among the things most hateful to God. Now, if this picture is not taken from the life; if the character of man is entirely different from that delineated in the Scriptures; or, if the vices of our nature are exaggerated; however difficult it may be to account for such misrepresentation, still it would furnish a strong argument against the inspiration of the writers of the several books of which the Bible consists. But on the other hand, if the character of man, as- given in the Scriptures, is found exactly to correspond with universal experience and observation, it will be an incontestable proof, that the writers were guided by a strict regard to truth, in their compositions. To enter into a particular consideration of this subject, does not comport with the plan of this work; but for the truth of the representations of Scripture, I would appeal to all authentic history, and to every man's own observation and experience. The description which the apostle Paul gives of the vices of the heathen world, in his time, is corroborated by all the historians and satirists who lived near that period. And who needs a labored proof, to show, that men have generally a tendency to be wicked? Every civil institution, and all the mist expensive provisions of civil government, are intended to set up barriers against the violence, injustice, and licentiousness of man. Indeed, civil government itself, originated in nothing else, than the necessity of protection against the wickedness of men. This, however, is a painful and mortifying conclusion; and it is not wonderful, that pride and self-flattery should render us reluctant to admit it; nevertheless, every impartial man must acknowledge, that our character is correctly drawn in the Bible.

There is something wonderful in the power, which the word of God possesses over the consciences of men. To those who never read or hear it, this fact must be unknown; but it is manifest to those who are conversant with the sacred volume, or who are in the habit of hearing it expounded. Why should this book, above all others, have the power of penetrating, and, as it were, searching, the inmost recesses of the soul, and shewing to a man, the multitude and enormity of the evils of his heart and life? This may, by some, be attributed to early education, but I believe, that if the experiment could be fairly tied, it would be found, that men who had never been brought up with any sentiments of reverence for the Bible, would experience its power over the conscience. The very best cure, therefore, for infidelity, would be, the serious perusal of the Holy Scriptures. "The entrance of thy word giveth light. The Law of the Lord is perfect, converting the soul."

3. It deserves our special attention, in considering the internal evidences of Christianity, that the Scriptures contain explicit information on those points, on which man stands most in need of instruction. These may be reduced to three: first., the doctrine of a future state of retribution; secondly, the assurance that sin may be pardoned, and the method by which this can consistently be done; and, thirdly, the means for restoring. the depraved nature of man, to a state of rectitude. We are not capable of determining, in particular, as we have before shown, what a revelation should contain, but it is reasonable to think, that if God gives a revelation, it will contain some instruction on these important

*Archibald Alexander, D. D.*

points.

And when we examine what the Scriptures teach, on these subjects, it is found, that the doctrine is worthy of God, and so adapted to the necessities of man, that it affords a strong argument in favor of their inspiration.

The certainty of a future existence to man, is a prominent feature in the New Testament. The connexion between our present conduct and future condition, is clearly and expressly inculcated. Many interesting and momentous truths, connected with the world to come, are presented in a light, the best calculated to make a deep and salutary impression on the mind. It is revealed, that there will be a general judgment of all then and that God hath appointed a day when this event shall take place. It is, moreover, taught, in the New-Testament, that not only will every man be judged, but every action of every individual, whether it be good or bad, will be brought under review; and that the eternal destiny of all men will be fixed, agreeably to the judicial decision of this impartial trial. Some will be admitted to everlasting life, in the world above, while others shall go away into. everlasting misery, into that place, "prepared for the devil and his angels."

Another interesting fact revealed in the New Testament, is, that there will be a general resurrection of the bodies of all men, previously to the final judgment. This fact, reason could never have conjectured: it must, from its nature, be a matter of pure revelation. We may, indeed, discover some remote analogy to the resurrection, in the apparent death and resuscitation of vegetables and some animals, but this could never have authorized, the conclusion that the bodies of men, after being mingled with the dust of the earth, would be reorganized and re-animated, by the same souls which were connected with them before their death. This doctrine, however, is very interesting; and to the pious, must be very pleasing and animating, as we may learn from the beautiful and striking description of the resurrection, given by Paul, "It is sown in corruption, it is raised in incorruption; it is sown in weakness, it is raised in power; it is sown a natural body, it is raised a spiritual body;--For this corruptible must put on incorruption, and this mortal must put on immortality."

It is worthy of remark, that although the Scriptures express the joys of heaven, and the miseries of hell, by the strongest figures, they do not enter much into detail, respecting the condition of men, in the future world. There is true wisdom in this silence; because it is a subject, of which we are, at present, incapable. of forming any distinct conceptions. Paul, after being caught up "to paradise, and to the third heaven," gave no account of what he saw and heard, when he returned. How different is this from the ridiculous description of the seven heavens, by Mohammed; and from the reveries of Emmanuel Swedenborg! The account of a future state, contained in the New Testament, is just that which is best suited to our present imperfect mode of conceiving; and at the same time, adapted to make the deepest impressions on the minds of men.

The method of obtaining the pardon of sin, which is made known in the Scriptures, is so extraordinary, and yet so perfectly calculated to reconcile the forgiveness of the sinner, with the justice and holiness of God, that it seems very improbable, that it is a mere human device. The mission from heaven, of a person called the Son of God; his miraculous assumption of human nature; his holy and benevolent. character; and his laying down his life as an expiation for the sins of men, are, indeed wonderful events, but on that account, not likely to be the invention of impostors. The death of Christ, may be considered the central point in the Christian system. This was so far from being an incidental thing, or an event occurring in the common course of nature, that it is, every where, represented to be the very purpose of Christ's coming into the world. This, according to the Gospel, is the grand means of obtaining all blessings for sinners. It is the great vicarious sacrifice, offered up to God in behalf of the people, in consequence of which God can be just and the justifier of all who believe in Jesus. To know Christ crucified, therefore, is to know the whole Gospel;--to preach Christ crucified, is to preach the whole Gospel;--for all its doctrines are involved in this event. The plan of salvation revealed in the Scriptures, is founded on the principle of receiving satisfaction for the transgressions of the sinner, from another person, who is able to render to the law all that is required from the offender This satisfaction was made by the obedience of Christ unto death, and is accepted by the Judge of all, in place of a perfect obedience of the sinner, in behalf of all those to whom it shall be applied. This method of obtaining pardon is honorable to God, because, while he receives the transgressor into favor, he expresses his hatred of sin in the strongest manner, and requires that the demands of his holy law be perfectly fulfilled; and it is suited to man, for it comes down to his impotence and wretchedness, and offers him a finished and gratuitous salvation, without works or merit of his own. And that there may be no room for an abuse of this doctrine of FREE GRACE, it is provided, that all who hope for the benefits of this redemption, shall yield a sincere obedience to the Gospel; and thus evince their penitence for their sins, and their love to the Saviour. Ungodly men may pervert this doctrine, and turn the grace. of God into licentiousness, but this receives no encouragement from the principles of the Gospel: it is merely the effect of the perverseness of sinful men.

This leads me to speak of the third thing, which was mentioned as important to be known by man, which is the means by which a depraved nature may be restored to rectitude; or in other words, how the

*The Evidences of the Christian Religion*

thorough reformation of a sinner may be effected. On this subject, philosophy has never been able to shed any light. And this is not wonderful; for the most that human wisdom if ever so perfect could effect, would be the direction and regulation of the natural principles and passions of men; but in this way no true reformation can be produced. Whatever changes are effected, will be only from one species of sin to another. In order to a radical restoration of the soul to moral rectitude, or to any degree of it, there is a necessity for the introduction, into the mind, of some new and powerful principle of action, sufficient to counteract or expel the principles of sin. It is in vain that men talk of producing a restoration to virtue, by reason: the mere perception of the right way will answer no purpose, unless there is some inclination to pursue it. Now, the want of virtuous affections, or to speak more correctly, of holy dispositions, is the great defect of our nature, in which our depravity radically consists; and the only way by which man can be led to lore and pursue the course of obedience to the law of God, is, by having love to God and to holiness excited, or implanted in his soul. But to effect this, is not in the power of any creature; it is a work which requires a divine energy--a creating power; and therefore a true conversion from the ways of sin, was never effected without supernatural aid. There may be an external reformation. There may be, and often is, a change of governing principles. The man who in his youth was under the predominant influence of the love of pleasure, may, in advanced years, fall completely under the control of avarice or ambition; but in every such case, the change is effected by one active principle becoming so strong, as to counteract or suppress another. It may be laid down as a universal maxim, that all changes of character are brought about by exciting, implanting, or strengthening, active principles, sufficient to overcome those which before governed the man.

Now let us inquire, what plan of reformation is proposed in the Scriptures. It is such a one, as precisely accords with the principles laid down. The necessity of regeneration, by the power of God, is taught almost in every variety of form, both in the Old and New Testament. The effect of the divine energy on the soul, is, A NEW HEART; or, new principles of moral action, the leading exercises of which are love to God, and love to man. Let a philosophical survey be taken of the nature of man, with his complete system of perceptions, passions, appetites, and affections; and then suppose this powerful and holy principle introduced into the soul, and it will be seen, that all the faculties and propensities of man, will be reduced to order; and the vices of our nature will be eradicated. Pretenders to reason and philosophy have often ridiculed this doctrine, as absurd; whereas, it is, in every respect, consistent with the soundest philosophy. It is the very thing which a wise philosopher, who should undertake to solve the problem, how depraved man might be restored to virtue, would demand. But like the foundation Archimedes required for his lever to raise the the principle necessary for a sinner's reformation, which reason and philosophy cannot furnish.

The Bible is the only book which ever taught the method of purifying the soul from sin. A thousand actual devices have been tried by philosophers, and es of other systems. One of the most common een, to endeavour to extricate the soul from the nce of the body, by various methods of mortification, and purgation; but all these plans have adopted lse principle, that the body is the chief seat of rity, and therefore they have ever proved unsuccessful. The disease lies deeper, and is further removed ... the reach of their remedies, than they supposed. he Gospel which teaches the true philosophy regarding the seat of sin, and its cure. Out of the heart d all evils, according to the Bible. And if we make the fruit good, we must first make the od.

This necessity of divine agency to make men truly us, does not, however, supersede the use of means, lude the operation of rational motives. When a principle is introduced into a rational soul, in the e of this principle, the soul is governed by the general laws of understanding and choice, as be The principle of piety is pre-eminently a rational le, in its operation. God is loved, because he is viewed to be a most excellent and amiable being. n is preferred to earth, because it is seen to be a ter and more enduring inheritance; and so of all exercises.

naturally led, from the consideration of this t, to speak of the moral system of the New Testament. I confine my remarks here, to the New Testament, not because it teaches a different rule of moral duty, from the Old, but because it teaches it more clearly.

I need say nothing in general commendation of the moral precepts of the Gospel. They have extorted the highest praise from many of the most determined enemies of Christianity. No man has been able to show how they could be improved in any one point. It has sometimes, indeed, been objected, that this system was not suited to man, because it requires a purity and perfection to which he can never attain; but the objection concedes the very point which we wish to establish,--namely, the absolute perfection of the Gospel system of morality. It surely requires no argument to prove, that if God revealed a rule for the regulation of his creatures, it will be a perfect rule. It will never do to admit, that the law must be lowered in its demands, to adapt it to the imperfection of creatures. This would be destructive of all law.

It has again been objected, that in the precepts of the New Testament, many splendid virtues, acknowledged by the heathen moralists, have been omitted. Patriotism, friendship, bravery, &c., have been specified as be. longing to this class. To which we reply, that so far as patriotism and friendship are moral virtues, they are included in the general precepts of the Gospel, which require us to love our fellow men, and do them good; and in those which command us to think of "Whatsoever things are lovely, whatsoever things are of good report;" but when the love of country, and the attachment to a friend, interfere with the general obligations of loving all men, they are no longer virtues, but vices.

The excellence of the moral system of the New Testament, will be manifest, if we consider,--

1. Its simple, yet comprehensive character. All moral duties which can be conceived, as obligatory on man, are here reduced to two grand principles, the love of God, and the love of man. The measure of the first is, the full extent of our capacity; of the second, the love which we have for ourselves. On these two, says Christ, hang all the law and the prophets. The duties which relate to temperance and self-government, do not need any additional principle. If the soul be filled with love to God, and with love to man, self-love will be so regulated and directed, as to answer every purpose in moving us to perform what has been called our duty to ourselves.

2. The precepts of morality, in the New Testament; although sometimes expressed in comprehensive language, are often applied to the actual relations and various conditions of men. We are not left to infer particular duties from general principles, but the duties of individuals, according to their circumstances, are distinctly enjoined. Parents and children, husbands and wives, magistrates and subjects, ministers and people, the rich and the poor, the friend and the stranger, have all their respective duties clearly marked out.

3. Moral duties which have been overlooked, or misunderstood, by other teachers, are here prominently exhibited, and solemnly inculcated. The virtues of humility, meekness, forbearance, and the forgiveness of injuries were not acknowledged by the heathen moralists; but in the New Testament they are made to assume their proper place, and much of true goodness is made to consist in their exercise. At the time of the advent of Christ, many false principles of morality had gained currency. The duty of loving all men, had been circumscribed within narrow limits. Men charged with heresy, as the Samaritans, or notorious sinners, as the Publicans, were, by the Jews, considered as properly excluded from all participation in their kindness, or courtesy. The duty of subjection to a foreign power, by which they had been conquered; and especially, the duty of yielding obedience to a wicked tyrannical prince, was one on which it required much wisdom to decide aright. The people were divided among themselves on this point; it was therefore selected by a combination of both parties, as a fit subject to entangle our Lord, by obliging him to decide one way or the other, and thus expose himself to the opposition of one of the parties. But when they asked him whether it was lawful to give tribute unto Cæsar or not, he called for a denarius, and looking at the image stamped upon it, asked whose it was; and upon being answered, Cæsar's, made the following remarkable reply, "Render unto Cæsar the things that are Cæsar's, and unto God the things that are God's." By which he decided, that, inasmuch as they permitted the coin of Cæsar to circulate among them, which was an evidence of his sovereignty over them, and availed themselves of this money for purposes of trade, there could be no impropriety in rendering to Cæsar what properly belongs to him; and, also, that this was not incompatible with their allegiance to God. So that, virtually, in this answer, he reproved both the Pharisees and the Herodians; the former, of whom made their duty to God a pretext for refusing to pay tribute to the Emperor; and the latter, to secure the favor of the reigning powers, neglected their duty to God.

Paul, living under the government of Nero, prescribes obedience to the existing powers, not from fear of suffering their displeasure, but "for conscience sake." This is the general rule of duty, on this difficult subject, than which none can be wiser; but it must not be considered, as inculcating passive obedience and nonresistance, in all cases. Yet, as long as a government has authority, so long we are bound to obey. Christianity is so constituted, as not to interfere with any civil institution. It takes men as it finds them, in all the relations of life, and teaches them their duty. It never can, therefore, be the cause of sedition, and opposition to existing governments. It considers all civil rulers, as the ministers of God, for the peace and good order of society, and for the punishment of those that do evil. It is made the duty of Christians, therefore, to be "subject unto the higher powers," and "not to resist the ordinance of God.--To render to all their dues; tribute to whom tribute is due, custom to whom custom, fear to whom fear; honor to whom honor." [44] --But when they who have the right to change the government, of a country, exercise it, and put down one set of rulers, and set up another, the principle of Christian duty remains the same. And if, in any country, Christians form a majority of the nation, there is no reason why they may not exercise this right of new modelling their government, or changing their rulers, as well as others.

4. The moral system of the New Testament traces all virtue to the heart, and sets no value on the most splendid and costly offerings, or the most punctilious discharge of religious duties, when the motives are not pure. The first inclination of the mind to an illicit object, is denounced to be a violation of the law; and words of reproach, and all idle words, are among the sins for which an account must be given in the Judgment. Prayers and alms, proceeding from vain glory, are represented as receiving no reward from God, however they may be applauded by men.

The love of this world, and the love of money, are represented as radical sins, from which many others proceed.

Pride and revenge are exhibited as not only odious, but incompatible with the divine favor. Purity of heart, and heavenly mindedness, with trust in God. and submission to his will, are; in this system, cardinal, virtues.

5. The moral precepts of the New Testament were exemplified in the lives of the apostles and primitive Christians; and especially, and to the utmost perfection, in the example of Jesus Christ. It is impossible to conceive a character more perfect than that given by the evangelists, of the Founder of the Christian religion; and it has already been observed, that this character, embracing every variety of excellence, often exhibited in delicate and difficult circumstances, is delineated by a simple narrative of facts. There is no panegyric; no effort or art to excite admiration; but the writers merely inform us what Jesus said, did, and suffered. From this narrative we learn, that he connected himself with no sect, and courted the favor of neither the rich nor the poor. He adopted none of the errors or prejudices of his nation; but by his discourses and his conduct, showed that he acted from far higher views than national prejudices. The apparent sanctity of the Pharisees, he denounced as hypocrisy;--the traditions of the elders, as subversive of the law of God;--the sceptical opinion of the Sadducees, as proceeding from ignorance of the true meaning of the Scriptures.

Jesus Christ continually turned the attention of his hearers, from earthly to heavenly things, as alone worthy of their affections and pursuit. Although he flattered no class of men, his attention was particularly directed to the poor; their spiritual necessities and their bodily afflictions excited his most tender compassion; and to them he addressed many kind and encouraging declarations. But his healing power was exerted in behalf of all applicants, rich and pool; and without regard to their sect or nation. Jews, Samaritans, Heathens, Publicans, and sinners, were the objects of his compassion. He was not deterred by the proud prejudices of the Scribes and Pharisees, from associating with penitents, however vile and infamous they had before been. He graciously received returning sinners, comforted them with the assurance of pardon, and permitted them to manifest their grateful affection to his person; by, the most expressive signs and actions.

He manifested the kindest sympathy with his friends in their afflictions, weeping with those that wept, and often exerting his omnipotence in raising their dear relations from the bed of sickness, or from death. And although he often uttered severe rebukes against the incorrigibly wicked, and was sometimes grieved and angry with them, yet his compassion towards them never failed; and even when their day of grace was ended, he wept over them with the most affecting tenderness.

Jesus Christ was often brought into conflict with insidious, malignant, and learned adversaries. They attacked him with deliberate craft, and. proposed to him questions on delicate and difficult subjects, to which he was required to return an immediate answer; but in no case of this sort was he ever confounded, or even puzzled by the cunning craftiness of his enemies. His answers were so appropriate, and so fraught with wisdom, that his adversaries were commonly confounded, and the audience filled with admiration.

The parables of Christ are unparalleled for beauty and force, in the species of composition to which they belong. But this is the smallest part of their excellence. They contain so much important truth, and so happily adapted to the subject, and the occasion, that often, the. persons intended to be reproved by them, were constrained to give judgment against themselves. In these discourses, the leading doctrines of the Gospel are exhibited in a beautiful dress of allegory, which rivets the attention, and greatly aids us in understanding the. fulness and freeness of the grace of the. Gospel. They are also prophetical of the rejection of the Jews, and of the calling of the Gentiles; of the various reception of the Gospel by different classes, of hearers; of the mixture of sincere and unsound Christians, of which the Church should consist; of the cruel persecutions which the followers of Christ should endure; and of the final overthrow and destruction of his enemies.

Jesus Christ spake, in all his discourses; as never man spake. He removed the false glosses which had been put on the law, and set its precepts in their proper light. He mingled the dogmas of no philosophical system with his instructions. He entered into no metaphysical and abstruse disquisition, but taught the truth with simplicity and authority.

His zeal for the honor of God, and for the purity and sanctity of his worship, and his dislike of all human inventions and will-worship, are manifest, in all his conduct. A spirit of fervent and, elevated devotion, was a remarkable characteristic of Jesus of Nazareth. Whole nights he spent in prayer; and before day he would retire for the purposes of devotion. He was in the habit of praying and giving thanks on all occasions; but his devotion was free from all tincture of superstition, or enthusiasm. He taught, that not the. words, but the heart;--not the length of prayers, but their, spirit, was regarded.

His benevolence, meekness, and laborious diligence, in promoting the welfare of men, were manifested, every day of his life. But in his acts of mercy, and in his most extraordinary miracles, there was no appearance of parade or ostentation. "He went about doing good," but he sought no glory from men. He was humble, retired, and contented with the lowest state of poverty.

When the people applauded him, he withdrew unto some other place. When they would have made him a king, he escaped from their hands. When they asked curious questions, he directed them to something important. When they uttered unmeaning expressions of praise, he took occasion to announce some important truth, or deliver some interesting discourse.

In nothing did he discover more profound wisdom,. than in declining to interfere, in any case, with temporal concerns, and disputes about earthly possessions. He showed by his conduct, what lie solemnly declared on his trial, that, "his kingdom was not of this world."

In his intercourse with his disciples, we observe a sweet mixture of dignity and gentleness, of faithfulness and humble condescension to their weakness and prejudices.. No wonder that they should love such a Master. But his last discourses with them before his passion, and the remarkable prayer offered in their behalf,.for affectionate tenderness, and the sweet spirit of consolation which pervade them, are altogether inimitable. How flat and unsatisfactory are the conversations of Socrates with his friends, when compared with those of Christ, recorded in the xiv, xv, and xvi chapters of the Gospel of St. John! Indeed, it would be impossible to refer to any discourses, in any language, which could bear a comparison with this valedictory of Christ: and that which should enhance our admiration of the pure benevolence of the author; is, that he was aware, that his own sufferings were near, and would be most cruel and ignominious; and yet his attention is turned to the case of his sorrowful disciples; and all that he says has relation to them. The institution of the Eucharistical Supper, intended to be commemorative of his death, was attended with circumstances, which exhibit the character of Jesus, in a very peculiar and interesting light. This scene will be best understood by a perusal of the simple and affecting narrative of the evangelists, to which the reader is referred.

The last thing in the character of Christ, which I shall bring into view at this time, is the patience and fortitude with which he endured sufferings, which were intense and overwhelming, beyond conception. There is something mysterious in this whole affair. The intense agonies which Jesus suffered, seem to have had no connexion with external circumstances. When he was betrayed, deserted, and arrested, he discovered no signs of fear or perturbation. He gave himself up, and submitted with unruffled composure, to every species of contumely and insult. While his trial was going on before the Sanhedrim, and before Pilate, he maintained, for the most part, a dignified silence, uttering no reproaches or complaints; not even speaking in his own defence. When particularly interrogated by the judges, he answered directly to the questions proposed, and avowed himself to be the Messiah, the Son of God, and the King of Israel. Under the mockery and insult which were heaped upon him, he remained perfectly composed, and uttered not a word indicative of impatience or resentment. "As a sheep before her shearers is dumb, so he opened not his mouth." When he was bewailed by the daughters of Jerusalem, as he ascended the hill of Calvary, bearing his cross, he requested them not to weep for him, but for themselves and their children, on account of the calamities that were coming on that devoted city. While suspended on the cross, he saw his beloved mother among the spectators, and knowing that she would need a friend and protector, he recommended her to the care of the. disciple he most tenderly loved. Although no compassion was mingled with the vindictive feelings with which he was persecuted, yet he set a glorious example of that most difficult duty, of loving our enemies: as says the apostle Peter, "Because Christ also suffered for us, leaving us an example, that ye should follow his steps: who did no sin, neither was guile found in his month; who, when he was reviled, reviled not again; when he suffered; he threatened not, but committed himself to him that judgeth righteously." Among his last words, before he expired, was a prayer for those that were then engaged in crucifying him;--"Father forgive them, for they know not what they do." A penitent thief, who was crucified with him, implored his blessing and remembrance, when he should come to the possession of his kingdom, to whom he replied, "This day shalt thou be with me in paradise." And finally, he said, "Father, into thy hands I commit my spirit," and bowed his head, and died.

The moral excellence of the character of Christ is very remarkable, for uniting in perfection, qualities which among men are considered almost incompatible, He exhibited a complete indifference to the possessions and glory of the world, and a devout and heavenly temper, without the least mixture of austerity. He combined uniform dignity, with humility and condescension:--manifested strong indignation against all manner of sin, and against impenitent sinners, but the most affectionate tenderness, towards every humble penitent. He united the spirit of elevated devotion also, with a life of activity and incessant exertion. While he held free intercourse with men of all classes, he adopted the prejudices, and spared the vices of none. On this subject, I will take the liberty of quoting a passage from an excellent discourse of Dr. Charming, referred to already: "I will only observe," says the eloquent author, speaking of the character of Christ, "that it had one distinction, which, more than any thing, forms a perfect character. It was made up of contrasts: in other words, it was a union of excellencies which are not easily reconciled, which seem at first sight incongruous, but which, when blended, and duly proportioned, constitute moral harmony, and attract with equal power, love, and veneration. For example, we discover in Jesus Christ an unparalleled dignity of character, a consciousness of greatness, never discovered or approached by any other individual in history; and yet this was blended with a condescension, loveliness, and unostentatious simplicity, which had never before been thought consistent with greatness. In like manner, he puked an utter superiority to the world, to its pleasures and ordinary interests, with suavity of manners, and freedom from austerity. He joined to strong feeling and self-possession, an indignant sensibility to sin, and compassion to the sinner; an intense devotion to his work, and calmness under opposition and ill success; a universal philanthropy, and a susceptibility of private attachments; the authority which became the Saviour of the world, and the tenderness and gratitude of a son."

The salutary effects of Christianity on communities and individuals, open a wide field for important remarks; but it is a subject which we have not time to pursue; yet we must not pass it over in entire silence. The argument from this topic may, however, be reduced to a point. Take a survey of the whole world, at this time, and let an impartial judgment be formed, of the condition of all the nations; and let the question be answered, whether Christian nations are in a less favorable, or more favorable condition, than others. And again, whether among Christians, those nations who have the free use of the Bible, and are carefully instructed in the doctrines of Christianity, are in a better or worse condition, than those to whom the Scriptures are interdicted, and who are permitted to remain in ignorance of the religion which they profess? The answers to these questions are so obvious, that I cannot but presume, that all readers will be of the same mind. It may then be asked, would a vile imposture be the means of meliorating the condition of the world, and prove salutary in proportion as it is known and obeyed? "I speak as unto wise men judge ye what I say."

We have, moreover, seen, in our own time, the wonderful effects of the Gospel, in civilizing some of the most barbarous people on the face of the earth. Men who seemed to be sunk to a level with the beasts, have been reclaimed, enlightened, and exalted, to a participation of the blessings of civilized life--their ferocious temper being completely subdued and softened. Look at Greenland, at Africa, at the islands in the Pacific; and nearer home, at the Cherokees, Choctaws, and other Indian tribes, and see what the Gospel can effect! I know not what infidels think of these things, but for my own part, I should not esteem one coming from the dead, or a voice of thunder from the heavens. so undoubted an evidence of the truth of .the Gospel, as these effects. Will a series of falsehoods produce such effects as these?

I know that it has been objected, that Christianity has been the cause of many bloody wars and cruel persecutions;--but this is impossible. That religion which breathes nothing but benevolence and peace, and which requires its disciples not to resist evil, but freely to forgive their most malignant enemies, never can be the cause of war and persecution. It may indeed be the occasion, and no doubt has been made the occasion. of such evils; but it would be absurd to attribute to Christianity, the evils of which it has been the innocent. occasion, when its own spirit is in direct opposition to those evils. As well might we charge civil government with all the wars and tumults which it has occasioned. As reasonably might we accuse liberty, as being the cause of all the atrocities of the French revolution. The truth is, that the wickedness of man is the cause of these evils; and the most excellent things in the universe, may be made the occasion of exciting, or calling it into exercise. Christ foretold that his religion would be an occasion of family discord; and to express the certainty of the event predicted, he said, "Think not not I am come to send peace on earth; I came not to send peace, but a sword; which some superficial readers have strangely misconstrued, as though he had signified, that it was the tendency of his religion to produce strife among friends. No man can remain in error on this subject who will take the pains to read the New Testament. And I will venture to predict, or rather to publish what is already predicted, that as soon as the world shall sincerely embrace the Christian religion, wars will cease to the ends of the earth. Then shall men beat their swords into plough shares, and their spears into pruning hooks, and learn war no more.

But the salutary effects of the Gospel on those individuals who cordially embrace it, furnish the most manifest proof of its divinity. flow often, by the secret, powerful influence of the truths of the Bible, have the proud been humbled; the impure rendered chaste; the unjust, honest; the cruel and revengeful, meek and forgiving; the drunkard, temperate; the profane, reverent; and the false swearer and liar, conscientious in declaring nothing but the truth! Under the influence of what other system are such salutary changes effected? Will it be said, that many who profess to experience such a change, prove themselves to be hypocrites? Admitted; but does this evince that they who give evidence of sincerity by the most incontestible proofs, all their lives, are also hypocrites? All men wish to be thought honest; but if many are discovered to be knaves, does this prove that there is not an honest man in the world?

But however this argument may affect those who have had no experience of the power of the Gospel, it will have great weight with all those who have, by means of the truth, been converted from the error of their ways. There are thousands who can attest that they have experienced the salutary efficacy of the Bible, in turning them away from their iniquities and enkindling within them the love of God, and of virtue. They cannot but believe that the Christian religion is from God, and are persuaded that no imposture could so elevate and sanctify the mind:--that no human device could possess such a power over the conscience and the heart, as they have experienced from the Scriptures. These persons,

*Archibald Alexander, D. D.*

therefore, may truly be said to have the witness of the truth in themselves.

But there is an efficacy in the truths of the Bible, not only to guide and santify, but also to afford consolation to the afflicted, in body or mind. Indeed, the Gospel brings peace into every bosom, where it is cordially received. When the conscience is pierced with the stings of guilt, and the soul writhes under a wound which no human medicine can heal, the promises of the Gospel are like the balm of Gilead, a sovereign cure for this intolerable and deeply seated malady. Under its cheering influence, the broken spirit is healed, and the burden of despair is removed far away. The Gospel, like an angel of mercy, can bring consolation into the darkest scenes of adversity; it can penetrate the dungeon, and soothe the sorrows of the penitent in his chains, and on his bed of straw. It has power to give courage to the heart, and to brighten the countenance of the man who meets death on the scaffold, or on the gibbet, if its precious invitations to the chief of sinners, be sincerely embraced. It mitigates the sorrows of the bereaved, and wipes away the bitter tears, occasioned by the painful separation of affectionate friends and relatives. By the bright prospects which it opens, and the lively hopes which it inspires, the darkness of the tomb is illumined; so that Christians are enabled, in faith of the resurrection of the body, to commit the remains of their dearest friends to the secure sepulchre, in confident hope, that after a short sleep, they will awake to life everlasting.

The cottages of the poor, are often blessed with the consolation of the Gospel, which is peculiarly adapted to the children of affliction and poverty. It was one of the signs of Jesus being the true Messiah, "that the poor had the Gospel preached unto them." Here, it produces contentment, resignation, mutual kindness, and the longing after immortality. The aged and infirm, who, by the gradual failure of their faculties, or by disease and decrepitude are shut out from the business and enjoyments of this world, may find in the word of God, a fountain of consolation. They- may, while imbued with its celestial spirit, look upon the world without the least regard for its loss, and may rejoice in the prospect before them, with a joy unspeakable and full of glory. The Gospel can render tolerable, even the yoke of slavery, and the chains of the oppressor. How often is the pious slave, through the blessed influence of the word of God, a thousand Limes happier than his lordly master! He cares not for the short deprivation of liberty; he knows and feels that he is "Christ's freeman," and believes "that all things work together for his good," and that "these light afflictions which are for a moment, will work out for him a fax more exceeding and eternal weight of glory!" But, moreover, this glorious gospel is an antidote to death itself. He that does the sayings of Christ shall never taste of death; that is, of death as a curse;--he shall never feel the envenomed sting of death. How often does it overspread the spirit of the departing saint, with serenity! How often does it elevate, and fill with celestial joy, the soul which is just leaving the earthly house of this tabernacle? It actually renders, in many instances, the bed of the dying, a place of sweet repose. No terrors hover over them;--no anxious care corrodes their spirit;--no burden oppresses their heart. All is light;--all is hope and assurance;--all is joy and triumph!

Now, the question to be decided is, whether a book which is replete with such sublime and correct views of theology;--which exhibits the true history and true character of man, without flattery, distortion, or exaggeration; and which possesses such an astonishing power of penetrating the human heart and affecting the conscience,--which gives us information on the very points, with which it is most important that we should be acquainted;--which opens to us the future world, and shows us how we may attain its felicity and glory;--which exhibits a perfect system of moral duty adapted to our nature and circumstances, and free from all the defects of other systems of morality; forbidding nothing which is innocent, and requiring nothing which is not reasonable and virtuous;--which reduces all duty to a few general principles, and yet illustrates the application of these principles by a multitude of particular precepts, addressed to persons in every relation of life, and exemplifies them, by setting before us the lives of holy men, who are portrayed according to truth, with such imperfections, as experience teaches us, belong to the best men;--which delineates the character of Jesus Christ, the founder of Christianity, with such a perfection of moral excellencies, by simply relating his words, actions, and sufferings, that nothing can be taken from it, or added to it, without detracting from its worth;--and finally, which contains the true sources of consolation for every species of human suffering, and comfort in death itself. I say, is it reasonable to believe, that such a book is the production of vile impostors; and especially, of uneducated fishermen of Galilee?

Would such men have fallen into no palpable blunders in theology or morality? Could they have preserved so beautiful a harmony and consistency between all the parts? Could they have exhibited such a character as that of Jesus Christ? and while they introduce him acting and speaking so often, and in circumstances so peculiar and difficult, never ascribe to him any error or weakness, in word or deed? Would impostors have denounced all manner of falsehood and deceit, as is done in the New Testament? Would they have insisted so much on holiness, even in the thoughts and purposes of the heart? Could they have so perfectly adapted their forgery to the constitution of the human mind, and to the circumstances of men? Is it, probable that they would have possessed the wisdom to avoid all the prejudices of their nation, and all connexion with existing sects and civil institutions? And finally, could they have provided so effectually for the consolation of the afflicted? What man now upon earth could compose even the discourses, said by the evangelists to have been spoken by Christ?

If any man can bring himself, after an impartial examination of the Scriptures, to believe that they were written by unprincipled impostors, then he may believe, that au untutored savage might construct a ship of the line; that a child might have written the Iliad, or Paradise Lost: or even that the starry firmament was the work of mere creatures. No: it cannot be, that this is a forgery. No man or set of men ever had sufficient talents and knowledge, to forge such a book as the Bible. It evidently transcends all human effort. It has upon its face the impress of divinity. It shines with a light, which from its clearness and its splendor, shows itself to be celestial. It possesses the energy and penetrating influence which bespeak the omnipotence and omniscience of its Author. It has the effect of enlightening, elevating, purifying, directing, and comforting all those who cordially receive it. Surely, then, it is the word of God, and we will hold it fast, as the best blessing which God has vouchsafed to man.

O precious gospel! Will any merciless liana endeavor to tear away from our hearts this best, this last, this sweetest consolation? Would you darken the only avenue through which one ray of hope can enter? Would you tear from the aged and infirm poor, the only prop on which their souls can repose in peace? Would you deprive the dying of their only source of consolation? Would you rob the world of its richest treasure? Would you let loose the flood-gates of every vice, and bring back upon the earth, the horrors of superstition, or the atrocities of atheism? Then endeavor to subvert the Gospel--throw around you the fire-brands of infidelity--laugh at religion, and make a mock of futurity;--but be assured, that for all these things, God will bring you into judgment. But no; I will not believe, that any who reflect on what has been said in these pages, will ever cherish a thought so diabolical. 1 will persuade myself, that a regard for the welfare of their country, if no higher motive, will induce them to respect the Christian Religion. And every pious heart will say, RATHER LET THE SUN BE DARKENED IN THE HEAVENS, THAN THE PRECIOUS LIGHT OF THE GOSPEL BE EXTINGUISHED!

## *Footnotes:*

40. Dr. Chalmers.
41. Soame Jenyns.
42. Chalmers' Evidences.
43. See Watson's Address to Scoffers.
44. Rom. xiii.

*Archibald Alexander, D. D.*

# CHAPTER XI - THE SCRIPTURES OF THE OLD AND NEW TESTAMENT, WERE WRITTEN BY THE INSPIRATION OF GOD; AND THIS INSPIRATION, HOWEVER IT MAY BE DISTINGUISHED, WAS PLENARY; THAT IS, THE WRITERS WERE UNDER AN INFALLIBLE GUIDANCE, 130TH AS IT RELATES TO THE IDEAS AND WORDS: AND YET, THE ACQUIRED KNOWLEDGE, HABITS, AND PECULIAR DISPOSITIONS OF THE WRITERS, WERE NOT SUPERSEDED

HAVING endeavored to establish the authenticty of the Scriptures, I come now to say something respecting the inspiration of the writers of the several books. These two subjects are, it is true, involved, in each other; and many of the arguments for the former, are conclusive in favor of the latter; but still, there is a distinction which it is important to observe. A book may be authentic, without having the least claim to inspiration, as are all true narratives of facts, written by men of veracity, in the exercise of their unassisted powers. The gospel history may be established on the common principles of human testimony, in the same manner, as any other history. Indeed, this must be done, in the order of proof, before any convincing argument can be formed, in favor of divine revelation. Accordingly, all judicious writers on the Evidences of Christianity, first attempt to establish the facts recorded in the Gospels, by an appeal to merely human testimony. This distinction is so clear, and practically so important, that many persons believe in the facts--miracles as well as others--and yet have no conviction that the history of these events was written by divine inspiration. This is understood to be the case in regard to most of those called Unitarians. Dr. Priestley, in his "Institutes of the Christian Religion," has established the authenticity of the facts, recorded by the evangelists, with great force of reasoning; and yet, in the same work, he utterly denies the plenary inspiration of these writers; but alleges, that they were men of veracity, and that their testimony should be received, just as we receive that of other credible historians; but without ascribing infallibility to them The same opinions have been maintained by many others. The authenticity of the facts is sufficient to demonstrate, that the Christian religion is of divine origin; but it does. not follow, as a matter of course, that the historian who gives an account of the facts orr which it rests, was inspired. This is a distinct inquiry; and, although, not so vitally important as the former, yet is of great moment, and deserves a serious and impartial consideration.

It may be proper, also, in this place, to distinguish between inspiration, and that illumination, which every true Christian must receive, and which is the foundation of that saving faith which is produced in the mind, by the operation of the Holy Spirit. The distinction is, that the object of inspiration is commonly to reveal some new truths; or more clearly to reveal such as were before but obscurely revealed; or, it is intended, to direct the mind, in a supernatural way, to write and speak certain things; and so superintends or strengthens its faculties, that it is enabled to communicate, with unerring certainty, truths before known; or, to form ideas and adopt expressions so sublime, as to be above the range of the natural powers of the person. But the illumination of the Holy Spirit communicates no new truths, but enables the soul spiritually to apprehend truths already revealed. Here then is the grand distinction between those spiritual influences which all Christians enjoy, and enthusiasm, which claims something of the nature of inspiration. The sober Christian can appeal to the

## The Evidences of the Christian Religion

word of God, as containing all the ideas by which his mind is affected, in its highest elevations of joy and love: but the enthusiast departs from the written word, and trusts to impulses, impressions on the imagination, immediate suggestions, dreams, or supposed visions. If these impulses or suggestions were from the Spirit of God, they would be strictly of the nature of inspiration. And, accordingly, most fanatics believe themselves to be inspired; but however strong their persuasion, we are not bound to believe in their pretensions, unless they can exhibit these external proofs, by which God is pleased to give attestation to those communications which he makes to men.

There is also a difference between inspiration, and revelation. All revelations are not made by a suggestion of truth to the mind of an individual. God often spike to people of old, by audible voices; and communicated his will by the missions of angels. Many persons have thus received divine revelations, who had no pretensions to inspiration. All the people of Israel, who stood before God at Mount Sinai, heard his voice, uttering the ten commandments, and yet no one would say, that all these were inspired. So, also, when Christ was upon earth, in more instances than one, a voice was heard declaring, that he was the beloved Son of God. Indeed, all who had the opportunity of hearing Christ's discourses, might be said to receive a revelation immediately from God; but it would be absurd to say, that all these were inspired. Dr. Dick is of opinion, that the word revelation would be more expressive, as being more comprehensive than suggestion, which last conveys the idea of an operation on the mind; whereas, truth, in many cases was made known, in other ways. But for the reasons stated above, it would not do to substitute the word revelation for inspiration; inasmuch as, multitudes received revelations, who had no claim to inspiration. And when inspiration is confined to those who wrote the books of Scripture, no other word would so clearly express the idea.

Inspiration has, by theologians, been distinguished into three kinds; that of superintendence, of suggestion, and elevation. The first of these takes place, when a historian is influenced, by the Holy Spirit, to write, and in writing is so directed as to select those facts and circumstances, which will answer the end proposed; and so assisted and strengthened in the narrative of events, as to he preserved from all error and mistake. The facts need not be revealed, because they may be well known to the writer from his own observation, and may be deeply impressed on his memory; but, no man can avoid inaccuracies and mistakes, in a narrative of facts, long past. If it is important that such a narrative be exempt from error, the writer must be inspired. But as the chief object of inspiration is, to communicate truths before unknown; so, the inspiration of suggestion is requisite, in all such eases; as when the prophets were inspired to predict the revolutions of empires; or, to communicate a message from God to a whole people, or to an individual, the ideas must of course, have been immediately suggested, by the Holy Spirit. The third species of inspiration, is, when, by a divine influence, persons are enabled to bring forth productions, in speaking or writing, far more sublime and excellent, than they could have attained, by the exercise of their own faculties. Thus, often, women, under the inspiration of God, have instantly uttered, in elevated strains of poetry, discourses in praise of God, which, by their unassisted powers, they could never have produced. In these compositions, there may be no revelation of new truth; nor is there a mere superintendence of the human faculties, as in the first case, was described; but the powers of the mind, are, for the occasion, wonderfully elevated above their common level, so that the conceptions are more vivid and sublime, and expressed in language more appropriate and striking, than would have naturally occurred to them. By an inspiration of this sort, David wrote the Psalms, and Solomon the Proverbs, and the Speakers in the book of Job, the sublime discourses, which are there recorded. Many things of this kind, are also found in the writings of the prophets.

Here, another question of some perplexity, demands our attention. It is, whether the words of Scripture, as well as the ideas, were given by inspiration. On the one hand, it is alleged, that there is no necessity for supposing that the words used in communicating revealed truth, should be suggested by the Holy Spirit; and that the fact proves that no such inspiration existed, because the style of each of the writers is peculiar, and accords precisely with his education, disposition, and turn of mind. But on the other hand, it is argued that unless the words were inspired, as well as the ideas we cannot be certain, that the writer has, in any case, communicated accurately, the mind of the Spirits; for, men are liable to mistake, in the selection of appropriate words, as much as in any thing else; and as men often fail in conveying their own ideas, in language which correctly expresses their meaning; so, also, they might make similar mistakes in the use of language, to express ideas received by inspiration; if in this matter they were left to the guidance of their own minds. It has also been plausibly urged in favor of inspiration extending to the words, that we can scarcely conceive of a revelation of truths to the mind, without supposing, that they were clothed in language. We cannot even think distinctly, much less reason conclusively, on any subject, without the intervention of words.

Now, it is probable, that, that has occured in this controversy, which has in many others; namely, that both parties are right; or, rather, that the truth will be fully possessed, by adopting the views entertained on both sides, and endeavoring to reconcile them. The fact is, that the same principles which apply to the ideas, may, without any alteration, be applied to the words. When the truths revealed were before unknown to the inspired person; and, especially--as seems often to have been the case with the prophets--when they did not fully comprehend the import of what was revealed, it is necessary to suppose, that the words, as well as ideas, were immediately suggested by the Holy Spirit. This was remarkably the case, when the apostles and others received the gift of tongues; which was nothing else but the inspiration of words, as they were needed, for the communication of the truths of the Gospel.

But as in the narration of well-known facts, the writer did not need a continual suggestion of every idea, but only to be so superintended, as to be preserved from error; in the use of language, in recording such familiar things, there existed no necessity that every word should be inspired; but there was the same need of a directing and superintending influence, as in regard to the things themselves. Here then, we see, that the language of the sacred writers might be preserved from impropriety, and inaccuracy; and yet, all the characteristics of style, peculiar to each writer, be retained. Just as if a master should so guide the hand of a child in writing, that the pen should be actually moved by the pupil; but governed and directed by the master, so as not to transgress the limits prescribed. Or, this superintendence, both as to ideas and words, may be illustrated, by the case of a father conducting a child along a narrow path. The child walks by its own activity, and takes steps according to its ability; but the father preserves it from falling, and keeps it in the straight path. Just so it is with men, when under the superintending influence of the Holy Spirit. Their own powers of understanding, memory, and invention, are not superseded, but only directed, and preserved from inaccuracy and error; but the man pursues his own peculiar method of thinking, reasoning, and expression. Ile speaks or writes in the language which he has learned, and uses that idiom and style, which have become habitual; so that inspired men, will, according to this theory, retain their peculiarity of style and expression, just as fully as if they were writing or speaking, without inspiration.

Some object to this theory of superintendence, under the impression, that it is less perfect, than if every thing was inspired by direct suggestion of the Holy Spirit. But there is really no foundation for this objection. It certainly is a matter of no consequence, how our knowledge is obtained, if only it is rendered infallibly certain. There are many things, concerning which we could not acquire a greater degree of assurance than we already possess, by inspiration of any kind: and such knowledge, acquired by the exercise of reason or intuition, is not the less valuable, because it has been obtained in a natural way. Indeed, these natural faculties, by which we are so constituted as to be capable of certain knowledge of the first principles of truth, are the gift of God, as much as any inspiration can be; and the clear intuitive knowledge, which we possess of certain truths, may be considered as a sort of permanent inspiration; for, suppose a man, by a constant plenary inspiration, to be made absolutely sure of the truth of certain propositions, so that he could not entertain any doubt respecting them, in what respect would there be any difference between this, and the intuitive perception of self-evident principles, which every rational man by nature possesses? There would, then, be nothing gained by the inspiration of direct suggestion, in regard to our knowledge of those things, of which we already possess intuitive certainty; so, it is also evident, that in relation to all our knowledge acquired by experience, or testimony, we only need such an influence, as will enable us to communicate what ought to be recorded, for the benefit of the church, and to do this without error, either as to matter or manner.

Some, who do not deny the inspiration of the sacred writers, in the general, have thought it necessary to make concessions on this subject, which are not called for, from the nature of the case, and have thus involved the cause which they defend, in real difficulties. They have granted, that while, in all matters of real importance, the penmen of the Scriptures were guided by a plenary inspiration; yet, in trivial matters, and the relation of unimportant circumstances, they were left to their own unassisted powers; and in such matters; have, therefore, fallen into mistakes, such as are incident to other honest historians, in similar circumstances. Now, no evil or inconvenience would result from this hypothesis, if the line could be definitely drawn, between the parts of the book, written by inspiration, and those in which the writers were left, to themselves. But as no human wisdom is sufficient to draw this line, the effect of this opinion is, to introduce uncertainty and doubt, in a matter, concerning which assurance is of the utmost importance. And it is in itself an improbable supposition, that the spirit of God should infallibly guide a writer in some parts of his discourse, and forsake him in other parts. If we find a witness mistaken in some particulars, it weakens our confidence in his general testimony. And could it be shown, that the evangelists had fallen into palpable mistakes, in facts of minor importance, it would be impossible to demonstrate, that they wrote any thing by inspiration.

The case of Paul is often adduced to prove, that a writer, who, for the most part, was inspired, may, in particular cases, be left to follow his own opinions.[45] If the meaning here ascribed to this apostle, and which, perhaps, is the most obvious, should be admitted, yet it. would riot authorise the opinion which we are now opposing. It would only follow, that in these few excepted cases, Paul was not inspired; which would leave us to enjoy full confidence in what he says, in all other cases, as being spoken by divine inspiration. But it may well be doubted, whether this was the true meaning of the apostle. It is much more probable, that all that he intended to teach, was, that our Lord Jesus Christ had delivered no opinion on the point which he was treating; but that he, by the aid of the spirit which was in him, expressed an opinion, which evidently he intended should be authoritative. And he plainly intimates, that be spoke by inspiration, when he says, "And I think also that I have the spirit of God." The import of this declaration, according to the usage of the New Testament, is, that Paul was persuaded that he was inspired, in uttering the sentiments which he did. The words "I think" should not be interpreted as signifying any doubt or uncertainty, for that is not at all the meaning of the original; but as being the expression of the conviction of his own mind. There is, therefore, no need to suppose, that Paul intended to intimate, that lie wrote any thing without the aid of divine inspiration. It would be strange, indeed, that lie who was inspired for all other purposes, should be left to himself in this one instance: and this is not to be reckoned among the least important matters which have fallen from his pen.

The true doctrine of inspiration then, is, SUCH A DIVINE INFLUENCE ON THE MINDS OF THE SACRED WRITERS, AS RENDERED THEM EXEMPT FROM ERROR, BOTH IN REGARD TO THE IDEAS AND WORDS.

This is properly called PLENARY inspiration. Nothing can be conceived more satisfactory. Certainty, infallible certainty, is the utmost that can be desired, in any narrative; and if we have this, in the sacred Scriptures, there is nothing more to be wished, in regard to this matter.

That the Scriptures of the Old Testament were appealed to, and constantly spoken of; as inspired, and as free from error, is capable of the clearest proof. Christ said to the Jews, "Search the Scriptures, for in them ye think ye have eternal life, but they are they which testify of me." "For had ye believed Moses, ye would have believed me, for he wrote of me." On another occasion, he said, "Ye do err, not knowing the Scriptures," where, it is evidently implied, that the Scriptures are an unerring rule. In the same chapter, it is recorded, that Jesus confounded the Pharisees by asking them, how David could, IN SPIRIT, call Christ, Lord, when he was his son. Again, Christ, after his resurrection, expresses his sentiment in the strongest terms: "These are the words which I spake unto you, while I was yet with you; THAT ALL THINGS MUST BE FULFILLED, which were written in the Law of Moses, and in the Prophets, and in the Psalms, concerning me. Then opened he their understandings, that they should understand the Scriptures; and said unto them, thus it is written, and thus it behoved Christ to suffer and to rise from the dead, on the third day." In the preceding part of the same discourse, this idea is also clearly exhibited. "Then he said unto them, O fools, and slow of heart to believe all that the prophets have spoken. Ought not Christ to have suffered these things, and to enter into his glory? And beginning at Moses and all. the prophets, he expounded unto them in all the Scriptures, the things concerning himself. And they said one to another, did not our hearts burn within us, while he talked with us by the way, and while he opened to us the Scriptures?" So, also, in the garden of Gethsemene, our Lord in addressing Peter, said, "Thinkest thou that I cannot now pray to my Father, and he shall presently give me more than twelve legions of angels? But how then shall the Scriptures be fulfilled, that thus it must be." The same infallible authority is ascribed to the Old Testament, by Christ, in his dispute with the Jews, recorded in the tenth chapter of John. "Jesus answered them, is it not written in your law, I said ye are gods? If he called them gods to whom the word of God came; and THE SCRIPTURE CANNOT BE BROKEN." We have, besides, many passages, in which the evangelists refer to the Holy Scriptures, as an infallible standard of truth. "But though he had done so many miracles before them, yet they believed not on him, that the saying of Esaias the prophet might be fulfilled, which he spake--Lord, who hath believed our report, and to whom is the arm of the Lord revealed?" "Therefore, they could not believe, because that Esaias said again--he hath blinded their eyes," &c. "For these things were done that the Scripture should be fulfilled, a bone of him shall not be broken. And again, another Scripture saith, they shall look on him whom they have pierced."

The apostles are not less explicit, in testifying to the inspiration of the Scriptures of the Old Testament, than Christ and the evangelists. Paul, in his second epistle to Timothy, puts him in mind, "that from a child he had known the Holy Scriptures, which were able to make him wise unto salvation, through faith which is in Christ Jesus;" and then adds, "All Scripture is given by inspiration of God, and is profitable for doctrine, for reproof, for correction, for instruction in righteousness; that the man of God may be perfect, thoroughly furnished unto all good works." The Scriptures, which Timothy knew from his childhood, must have been the books of the Old Testament, for, at that time, no others had been written: but when Paul goes on to declare, that "all Scripture was given by inspiration of God," he might have included under this general expression, all the books of the New Testament, which had been published, before his second imprisonment at Rome; and this would comprehend, probably, the first three Gospels, the Acts of the Apostles, and all his own epistles, besides; for this seems to have been the last of Paul's writings; for in the close of this epistle, he says, "For I am now ready to be offered, and the time of my departure is at hand." And that, about this time, the writings of Paul were, by the Church, reckoned among the sacred Scriptures, we learn from the second epistle of Peter, which was probably written about this time, or a little before. His words are remarkable, as containing the only clear testimony, on record, of one apostle, to the writings of another. "And account," says he, "that the long suffering of our Lord is salvation, even as our beloved brother Paul also, according to the wisdom given unto him, hath written unto you. As, also, in all his epistles, speaking in them of these things; in which are some things hard to be understood; which they that are unlearned and unstable pervert, as they do also the other Scriptures, to their own destruction." Hence, it would appear, that Paul's epistles were now well known, and were reckoned among the other Scriptures, by the apostle Peter. Certainly, then, Paul himself might have included them, as well as the other published books of the New Testament, under the phrase "all Scripture;" and if so, this passage will contain a strong testimony to the inspiration of the whole of the Old Testament, and a large part of the New Testament. And admitting the facts, of Paul's miraculous conversion, divine mission as an apostle, and that he was richly endowed with the gifts of tongues, of healing, of prophecy, &c., we cannot deny that he is a witness, in this case, on whom we may repose the most perfect confidence.

The apostle Peter has also given the most unequivocal testimony, to the inspiration of the prophets who penned the Old Testament. He had been speaking concerning the wonderful scene of which he was a witness, on the mount of transfiguration, whereupon, he goes on to say, "We have a more sure word of prophecy, whereunto ye do well that ye take heed, as unto a light that shineth in a dark place, until the day dawn, and the day star arise in your hearts; knowing this first, that no prophecy of Scripture is of any private interpretation. For the prophecy came not in old time by the will of man; but holy men of God spake as they were moved by the Holy Ghost." There is another testimony of this apostle, in his first epistle; in which he clearly speaks of the inspiration of the prophets. "Of which salvation the prophets have inquired, and searched diligently, who prophesied of the grace that should come unto you; searching what, or what manner of time, the Spirit of Christ which was in them did signify, when it certified beforehand the sufferings of Christ, and the glory that should follow. Unto whom it was revealed, that not unto themselves but unto us, they did minister the things which are now reported unto you, by them that have preached the Gospel unto you, with the Holy Ghost sent down from heaven."

That the Scriptures of the Old Testament were continually recognized by 4he apostles, as given by inspiration of God, is so evident from every mention of them, that it may seem to be a waste of time, to adduce the testimonies; but the subject is exceedingly important, and we cannot too frequently have these evidences set before our eyes.

In the epistle to the Hebrews, there are many clear testimonies, some of which I will bring forward. In the very first sentence, it is said, "God, who at sundry times, and in divers manners, spake in time past unto the fathers by the prophets, hath in these last days, spoken unto us by his Son." Whatever is spoken by the prophets is represented throughout this book, as spoken by God himself. Thus, in the same chapter, it is declared, "And when he bringeth the first begotten into the world, HE saith, And let all the angels of God worship him. And to the angels, HE saith, who maketh his angels spirits--but to the Son, HE saith, thy throne O God is for ever and ever." Now, all these passages, where God is said to speak, are quotations from the Psalms. Certainly then, we may conclude, that whatever is spoken in this book of Psalms, is from the inspiration of God. The same is the fact, in the next chapter, where a large part of the eighth Psalm is quoted, and applied to Christ. So, also, the Captain of our Salvation is represented as saying certain things, which are found written in the Old Testament. "Saying, I will declare thy name unto my brethren"--"And again, I will put my trust in him." And in the third chapter of this epistle, we have a quotation from the Psalms in the following remarkable words, "Wherefore, as the Holy Ghost saith, To-day if ye will hear his voice, harden not your hearts." And in the fourth chapter, the same style is used as before." For HE spake in a certain place of the seventh day, in this wise, and God did rest the seventh day from all his works." And in the fifth. "But HE said unto him, thou art my Son, to day have I begotten thee. As he saith also in another place, thou art a priest, forever after the order of Melchisedek." And God is represented as the speaker; not only in what is written in the Psalms, but in the prophets also. Thus, in the eighth chapter, we have a long quotation from Jeremiah, which is declared to be, the word of the Lord. "Behold the days come saith the Lord," &c. One more testimony from this book shall suffice. In the tenth chapter, it is said, "Wherefore the Holy Ghost also is a witness unto us; for after that he had said before, this is the covenant that I will make with them after those days, saith the Lord."

Nothing can be more evident then, than that as the writers of the Old Testament declared themselves to speak what they received from the Lord, so the whole of the Scriptures are continually referred to, and recognized, as given by inspiration; insomuch, that it would he difficult to find a single passage, in which these Scriptures are mentioned, in which this idea is not expressed, or clearly implied. And it will be shown, hereafter, that the writers of the New Testament claim inspiration for themselves.

If, as has been shown, the Old Testament was written by inspiration, and if the New Testament contains a revelation from God, not less important; and which, in fact, is the completion of the Old, can we believe, that. while prophets were inspired to write the former, the latter was left to be marred and obscured, by the weaknesses of uninspired men?

To accomplish the purpose intended by revelation, it seems necessary, that the writers who communicate it to posterity, should be guided by inspiration. The end of revelation is, to convey to men, a certain knowledge of truth, to guide their faith and practice. But if the book which contains such a revelation, is composed by erring, fallible men, we never can be sure, in any particular case, that we are in possession of the truth revealed. The men may be honest and faithful, but we know that all men are liable to errors and mistakes; and all men are more or less under the influence of prejudices and prepossessions. It is evident, therefore, that the purpose of giving a revelation, would be, in a great measure defeated, unless inspired men were employed to make the record by which it is to be transmitted to the various nations of the earth, and to posterity.

Again, when we carefully consider the subject matter of the books of the New Testament, we cannot repose implicit confidence in what is taught, unless we have evidence that the pens of the writers were under the guidance of inspiration. To record the discourses which a man hears, and transactions which he sees, seems, at first sight, to require nothing more than veracity and integrity, in the historian. This might, to a certain extent, be admitted, if the witness instantly noted down what he heard, or saw; but who can believe, that after the lapse of eight, fifteen, or fifty years, the evangelists would be able to record, with perfect accuracy, long discourses of their Master; and, to relate correctly, all the circumstances of the miracles, of which they have given an account? It may be said, indeed, that they could give, substantially, the facts of which they were witnesses; but this is far from being satisfactory. Such a record would lose a portion of that reverence which it ought to receive, to give it a commanding authority over the conscience, and to be a solid foundation for unshaken confidence, And in regard to mysterious and sublime doctrines, which the apostles teach in their epistles, if once we admit the idea, that they were fallible men, we shall continually be liable to doubt;--we shall be afraid that they have misapprehended, or forgotten, what they had heard: or, that under the bias of prejudice or inclination, they may have been led, insensibly, to give a distorted view of the truths which they inculcate.

But we are not left to conclude, from the necessity of the case merely, that the writers of the New Testament were inspired, by the Holy Ghost. We have clear and abundant proof, that our blessed Lord promised infallible guidance to his disciples, whom he chose to be his witnesses to the world; and to whom he committed the propagation of his religion, through all nations, and all ages, "And I will pray the father, and he shall give you another Comforter, that he may abide with you forever: even the spirit of truth, whom the world cannot receive because it seeth him not, neither knoweth him; but ye know him, for he dwelleth with you, and shall be in you." And that the Holy Spirit here promised, was to guide the apostles in delivering their testimony, may be inferred from what is said in the xv. chapter. "But when the COMFORTER is come, whom I will send unto you from the Father, even the Spirit of truth, which proceedeth from the Father, he shall testify of me. And ye shall bear witness, because ye have been with me from the beginning." The promise of plenary inspiration is, however, more explicitly given, in the xvi. chapter of John. "Howbeit, when he the Spirit of truth is come, HE WILL GUIDE YOU INTO ALL TRUTH; for he shall not speak of himself; but whatsoever he shall hear, that shall he speak; and he will show you things to come. He shall glorify me; for be shall receive of mine, and shall show it unto you. All things that the father hath are mine; therefore, said I, that he shall take of mine, and shall show it unto you." Christ also promised the inspiration of immediate suggestion to his disciples, when called to answer before kings and rulers, and commanded them not to premeditate what they should say, for it would be given to them at the moment what they ought to say, "For," said he, "It is not you that speak, but the Holy Ghost who speaketh in you." Now we may argue, with irresistible force, if plenary inspiration was granted to the apostles to enable diem to make a proper defence, when arraigned at a human tribunal, surely they would not be abandoned to their own weakness, when preparing a record of Christ's words and actions, which was, through all ages, to be the guide of his church? If the apostles were ever inspired, we may be sure that it was, when directed to finish and record the testimony of God. The very idea, that every book of the Old Testament was given by inspiration, but that the whole of the New was composed without this aid, is revolting to the reason of man. And this will appear the more unreasonable, when we consider, that the light of the new dispensation is seven-fold clearer than that of the Old. The very forerunner of Christ, was superior to all the prophets that preceded him: but the least in the kingdom of heaven was greater than he. Then, certainly, if all the prophets only spoke as they were moved by the Holy Ghost, the apostles, who were the chosen witnesses of Christ, and chief officers of his kingdom, were not left without this infallible guidance, when engaged in performing the most important part of the responsible duty assigned them; when executing that part of their commission, which was most effectual in extending and perpetuating his spiritual kingdom? Accordingly, the apostles claim to be inspired men; and speak with an authority which would be arrogant, if they had not written under an infallible guidance. They do not merely express their own private opinions, and endeavor to support them by argument; but they speak as men assured of the truth of what they deliver; and decide with authority and without hesitation, questions, which none but men inspired by the Holy Spirit could undertake thus positively to determine, without, exposing themselves to the charge of dogmatism and self-sufficiency.

Besides, some parts of the New Testament--like much of the old--are prophetic; and if true, could be written in no other way, than by inspiration. The Apocalypse, or Revelation given to John, is either a mere enthusiastic fable, or, it was written by inspiration; and such is the majesty of the ideas here presented, and the awful sublimity of the style, that even Dr. Priestly, was constrained to acknowledge, that it bore on its face, marks of a superhuman origin. And if we bad time to compare the prophetic representations .of this singular book with authentic history, there would arise an evidence of its inspiration, which could not be easily contradicted. Such men as, Sir Isaac Newton, Dr. Clarke, bishop Hurd, bishop Newton, and a multitude of others, have seen in this book, the most convincing .proof of divine inspiration. The same may be said of all the prophecies of the Old and New Testament. if there is any truth, whatever, in them, they must be inspired; for, none but inspired men can foretell future, contingent events. Indeed, in all the cases, where Moses and others declare, that God spoke to them, and communicated instructions, or laws, they must be considered as divinely directed, unless we deny their veracity. But we are now reasoning on the hypothesis, that the books are authentic, and written by men of truth and honesty.

The style of the evangelists has often been adduced as an evidence of their inspiration. Not that they write with an elegance and sublimity which cannot be imitated; but because they write as persons divested of the feelings which commonly belong to men. They write with an unaffected simplicity, and with an impartial, dispassionate regard to truth, that has no parallel, and has never been successfully initiated. How could illiterate men produce such works as the Gospels, without inspiration? Select a thousand sensible men, but unaccustomed to composition, and set them to write a simple history of the most remarkable transactions with which they have been conversant, and there will not be in any one of them, an approximation to the characteristic manner of the evangelists. Others, and men possessed of more learning than the apostles, have undertaken, without inspiration, to write Gospels, as if composed by some one or other of these holy men; but you cannot place the evidence of the inspiration of the genuine Gospels, in a stronger light, than by contrasting them with any, or all the apocryphal writings, under the names of the apostles.

But we are in danger here of repeating what has already been said, under the head of the Internal Evidences of Christianity. The truth is, that the whole of the arguments from this source, for divine revelation, are directly in point, to prove the doctrine of inspiration; and, therefore, instead of going over the ground a second time, I would refer to what has been said, in the preceding chapter.

Miracles, also, furnish the most conclusive proof of inspiration, where it can be ascertained, that the writer of any book of Scripture possessed the power of performing such works; for, the very end for which miracles were exhibited, was to prove that the person speaking was sent from God, to deliver some message. As Nicodemus properly said, "We know that thou art a teacher come from God, for no man can do the miracles which thou doest, unless God be with him." Well, if miracles are sufficient to prove the truth of an oral communication, will they not also be equally conclusive, in favor of a written declaration? If there be any difference, it is in favor of the latter, because it is much more important, that a written discourse, intended for the instruction of all ages, should be well attested, than a discourse from the lips, which is heard by few, and can never be recovered after it has been spoken.

In the whole of what has been said on the subject of inspiration, the truth of the facts recorded in the New Testament has been taken for granted; and, also, that the Scriptures contain a divine revelation. We are not arguing with infidels, but with those, who, while they acknowledge the divine origin of the Christian religion, doubt, or deny, that the persons who wrote the books of the Old and New Testament, were guided by a plenary inspiration. Now, as these persons admit that the apostles and evangelists were men of veracity and integrity, their testimony, on this subject, ought to be decisive. If they claim inspiration, we cannot deny it to them, without invalidating all the strongest evidences of the truth of Christianity. Why were they endowed with the power of working miracles, but that full credence might be given to what they testified; and when they declare, that they were moved by the Holy Ghost; and that what they delivered, was not the word of men but the word of God, received by divine revelation, do not these miraculous powers which they possessed, as fully confirm what they wrote, as what they spoke?

Having before shown, that the apostles furnish ample testimony to the inspiration of the Old Testament, we shall now adduce a few texts to prove, that they claimed inspiration for themselves. Their message is every where called THE WORD OF GOD; and Paul declares, that what he preached, he received not from man, but "from the revelation of Jesus Christ." that the things which he wrote, were "The commandments of the Lord;" and that the things which he and his brethren taught, "God had revealed them to them by his Spirit." He, therefore, declared, "He who despiseth the things which he taught, despised not men but God." Peter ranks "the commandments delivered by the apostles, with the words of the Holy Prophets; and as has been before remarked, reckons the epistles of Paul, with the other Scriptures." John says, "We are of God; he that knoweth God heareth us; he that is not of God, heareth not us. Hereby know we the spirit of truth, and the spirit of error."

The only thing wanting to complete the evidence of the inspiration of the New Testament, and consequently that of the Old, is to show, that these writings were received unanimously by the Christian Church, as inspired writings. But although, there exists abundant evidence of this fact, yet to pursue it would lead., us too much into detail, and would not comport with the studied brevity of this work. And I am the less inclined to enter on the labor of collecting this testimony, here, because I have attempted

*The Evidences of the Christian Religion*

this in another work. I may say, however, that in the early ages of the Church, no Christian ever called in question the inspiration of the sacred volume; but all held this as a fundamental point, in their religion. It was left for those, who chose to style themselves rationalists, in modern times, to admit the authenticity of the facts recorded in the Bible; while they utterly deny the plenary inspiration of the writers. But this is ground on which no consistent reasoner can long stand. The truth is, if the miracles and prophecies of the Scriptures be acknowledged, and the divine origin of Christianity be admitted, the inspiration of the penmen of these books must follow as a corollary. It cannot be denied without the greatest inconsistency. And, on the other hand, if inspiration be denied, the authenticity of the miracles and prophecies will soon Le abandoned. The course of theological opinion among the neologists of Germany, for a number of years past, furnishes a striking illustration of the truth of the aforesaid observations. For a while, the assault, in that country, was merely upon the doctrine of inspiration; but no sooner was that ground conceded, than the critics directed their artillery against the authenticity of the miraculous facts and prophecies.

There is no end to the objections which may be started against the plenary inspiration of the Scriptures, just as is the fact in regard to the visible universe, as. the work of God; and it cannot be denied, that there is a striking analogy between the mode of reasoning pursued by atheists and deists. But the foundation of all their arguments is human ignorance and they cannot, form the conception of a creation, by a Being of almighty power and infinite wisdom, and of a supernatural revelation from such a being, which would not be liable. to as great, and much greater objections, than they are able to bring forward against his works and word, as they do actually exist. If such men could be induced,. in a calm and unprejudiced manner, to examine this subject, I would recommend to them a careful perusal of Butler's Analogy, between Natural and Revealed Religion; and to the deist, I would especially recommend the seventh chapter, of the second Part, where. the author, in a manner peculiar to himself, makes first, some observations ON THE PARTICULAR EVIDENCES OF CHRISTIANITY, and then, in the close, exhibits a view of the evidence arising from a general survey of the contents of the Bible. The argument, as presented in this last form, is so original and striking, that I would insert it in this place, were I not afraid of swelling this volume to an inconvenient size. The whole of the second book of the Analogy may be considered as the most satisfactory method of meeting the popular objections to divine revelation, which was ever adopted.

And in regard to particular objections, arising from apparent discrepancies, from extraordinary facts, and from mysterious doctrines, found in the sacred volume, it will be sufficient to refer the inquisitive reader, to the first volume of Horne's Introduction, and to Dr. Dick's deservedly popular work, on Inspiration; and also, to learned commentators, some of whom have taken much pains to reconcile seeming contradictions, and to elucidate obscure passages, by an application of the rules of sacred criticism. I would only further remark, in relation to the usual objections to the inspiration of the Scriptures, that they militate as fully against the authenticity of the facts, as against, the inspiration of the writers; and, therefore, do not require to be considered and obviated under this head.

A summary of the whole evidence for the plenary inspiration of the Scriptures, of the Old and New Testament, is as follows:--All the Internal Evidences of Christianity, whether arising from the peculiar excellence of the matter, or the simplicity and sublimity of the style--from the perfection of the character ascribed to Jesus Christ--from the continual recognition of the over-ruling Providence of God--from the pure and elevated spirit of devotion which breathes through the sacred pages--from the penetrating and transforming efficacy of the Holy Scriptures--and from, their adaptation to the constitution of the human mind,. and to the existing relations among men;--go to prove, that they were written under the infallible guidance of the Holy Spirit.

Again, every prophecy which has been fulfilled, furnishes undoubted and independent evidence of the inspiration of that particular part of the Scriptures; and all the laws which proceeded from the mouth of Jehovah, must be considered as infallible precepts, unless we should call in question the whole truth of the narrative.

The writers, for the most part, were endued with the power of working miracles. These facts, it is admitted, prove that God spake by them; and if the: prophets and apostles were inspired in the discourses, which they delivered, then a fortiori, they must have been inspired in preparing those writings which were intended to guide the faith and practice of believers, through all ages.

Moreover, the sacred writers, generally lay claim to inspiration. They speak authoritatively in the name of the Lord. They call their message, the WORD OF GOD and Christ has set his seal to the plenary inspiration of all the Scriptures of the Old Testament. The apostles and evangelists, in the most explicit manner; declare the same truth.

Besides, Christ promised plenary inspiration to his disciples; and they professed to be under the guidance of the Spirit, in what they wrote.

And, finally, while some of the apostles were living, their writings were classed with the divine Scriptures; and were universally received as inspired, and as the infallible word of God, by the whole primitive Church.

*Archibald Alexander, D. D.*

We cannot but conclude, therefore, that all the books of the Old and New Testament, were written by the inspiration of God; and contain an infallible rule, to guide the faith and practice of the church, to the end of the world.

Footnote:
45. See 1 Cor. vii. 12-40.

# NOTES

## NOTE A - AN APPENDIX TO CHAPTER VI

*On the Proof of Miracles by Testimony.*

IN a recent popular, but anonymous publication, entitled, Essays on the Pursuit of Truth, on the Progress of Knowledge, and the Fundamental Principles of all Evidence and Expectation, By the Author of Essays on the Formation and Publication of Opinions," the doctrine of ne, on the subject of testimony, has been exhibited in a ...a somewhat new and imposing, And as this writer has ired considerable celebrity in England, and his Essays have been republished in Philadelphia, and recommended strongly to the public, upon the authority of the Westminster Review, it seems necessary to guard the public against the insidious design of these Essays; which we have reason to think, was not known to those concerned in the republication of the work in this country. Indeed, the ingenious author, never brings the subject of divine revelation directly into view, in all that he has written; and I believe, the word "miracles" does not occur in either of the volumes which he has published nevertheless, it is a fact, that in the last of his essays, he has revived, in substance, the famous argument of Hume, on miracles; and has, with even more concealed istry; than that celebrated infidel employed, endeavored to e that no testimony, however strong, is sufficient to establish fact which involves a deviation from the regular course of the laws of Nature. But that I may not be suspected of misrepresenting the sentiments of this discriminating and popular writer, I will here insert an extract, from the Essay before-mentioned, which contains the substance of the whole argument.

"But it is only a small part of our knowledge of past events which we gather from physical evidence. By far the most important source of information of such events is the testimony of human beings; and it is a curious, interesting, and momentous inquiry, whether we proceed on the same principle when we avail ourselves of this moral evidence to penetrate into the past, as when we make use of that which is of a purely physical character.

"Testimony must be either oral or written. As far as the mere physical circumstances are concerned, we evidently commence our use of it by reasoning from effects to causes. We infer, for example, that the writing before us has been the work of some human being, in doing which we of course assume the uniformity of causation. If from the circumstances attending the testimony we infer that is entitled to be received as veracious; if for instance, we find that it has proceeded from a man of tried integrity, and who acted under the influence of motives which render it unlikely that he should deceive, our inference still proceeds on the assumption of the same principle. I may have in other cases found these circumstances to have been the precursors or causes of true testimony; but how can I or any one tell that they have operated in the same way in the instance before me? The reply must evidently I be, that it is impossible to avoid assuming that the same causes have invariably the same effects.

"In fact, if we examine any of the rules which have been laid down for the reception of testimony, or any of those marks which have been pointed out as enabling us to judge of its credibility, we shall find them all involving the uniformity of causation. It is allowed on all hands, that the concurrence of a number of witnesses in the same assertion, their reputation for veracity, the fact of the testimony being against their own interest, the probability of detection in any false statements, are all circumstances enhancing the credibility of what they affirm. These are considered as general principles on the subject gathered from experience, and we apply them instinctively to any new case which may be presented to us, either in the course of our own observation, or as having taken place at some former period. But it is obvious from what has just been said, that unless we assume a uniformity in the succession of causes and effects, we cannot transfer our experience from any one case to another. That certain circumstances have produced true testimony in one or a hundred instances, can be no reason why they should produce it in a different instance, unless we assume that the same causes have necessarily the same effects.

"It is clearly shown by this reasoning, that in the reception of testimony and the use of physical evidence we proceed on the same principle. But in the case of testimony there is a peculiarity not belonging to physical evidence. In the former we not only have certain effects from which it is our task to infer the causes, or certain causes from which to infer the effects; as when we judge the writing before us to have been the work of some human being, or the testimony to be true on account of the circumstances under which it was given; but the testimony itself consists of the assertion of facts, and the nature of the facts asserted often forms part of the grounds on which the veracity of the testimony is determined; it frequently happens, that while external circumstances tend to confirm the testimony, the nature and circumstances of the facts attested render it highly improbable that any such facts should have taken place, and these two sets of circumstances -may be so exactly equivalent as to leave the mind in irremediable doubt. In the consideration of both, however, the same assumption is involved. We think the facts improbable, because we have found them rarely occurring under the circumstances stated; we think the testimony likely to be true, because we have generally found true testimony to proceed from witnesses acting under the influence of similar motives, and what we have found to happen in other cases we are irresistibly led to conclude must also happen in the case before us.

"The opposition of the circumstances of the evidence and the nature of the facts may be carried still further. Assertions are frequently made which in themselves imply a breach of the uniformity of causation. From such cases the conclusions already established remove all difficulty. To weigh probabilities, to determine what credit is due to two sets of conflicting circumstances, neither of which as far as our knowledge extends is irreconcilable to the usual course of nature, is often a nice and arduous task; but if the principles of this essay are correct, it is easy to see what reception ought to be given to assertions professedly implying a deviation from the uniform succession of causes and effects.

"Suppose, for instance, any person to affirm that he had exposed a cubic inch of ice to a temperature of 200 degrees of Fahrenheit, and that at the expiration of an hour it had retained its solidity. Here is a sequence of events asserted which is entirely at variance with the admitted course of nature; and the slightest reflection is sufficient to show that to believe the assertion would involve a logical absurdity. The intrinsic discrepancy of the facts could never be overcome by any possible proofs of the truth of the testimony.

"For let us put the strongest case imaginable; let us suppose that the circumstance of the ice remaining unmelted, rests on the concurrent testimony of a great number of people, people too of reputation, science, and perspacity, who had no motive for falsehood, who had discernment to perceive and honesty to tell the real truth, and whose interests would essentially suffer from any departure from veracity. Under such circumstances false testimony it may be alleged is impossible.

"Now mark the principle on which this representation proceeds. Let us concede the positions, that what is attested by a great number of witnesses must inevitably be true,--that people of reputation and intelligence without any apparent motive for falsehood are invariably accurate in their testimony, and that they are above all, incapable of violating truth, when a want of veracity would be ruinous to their interests. Granting all this, I ask the objector, how he knows that these things are so; that men of this character and in these circumstances speak truth? He will reply that he has invariably found them to act in this manner: but why, because you found them to act in this manner in a few or even in many cases, within your own experience or in the experience of ages, do you conclude that they have acted so in all cases and in the case before us? The only answer is, that it is impossible not to take for granted, that in precisely similar circumstances similar results will ensue, or that like causes have always like effects.

"Thus on the ground of the uniformity of causation, he would be maintaining the competency of testimony to prove a fact which implies a deviation from that uniformity."

Now it will abbreviate the answer to this specious argument, to acknowledge, that the general principle which this author takes so much pains to establish, and on which he builds his reasoning, is freely admitted, to be not only correct, but self-evident. That the same causes uniformly produce the same effects, is a truth so obvious, and so generally admitted, that it. was unnecessary for the ingenious author of this essay, to spend so much time in rendering it evident. And I am willing to admit its certainty to be as undoubted in moral, as in physical subjects. But while I freely admit, that the same causes will uniformly be followed by the same effects, I do by no means accede to the proposition, which our author seems to consider as of the same import; namely, that the course of nature, or the laws of nature, never have been interrupted, or suspended; and the whole appearance of force and plausibility which the argument of this writer possesses, arises from the artful confounding of these distinct propositions. I agree, that no testimony can be strong enough to induce a rational man to believe that the same causes will not be attended with the same effects: for this would be to assent to an evident absurdity. But it is an entirely different thing to believe, that the laws of nature have sometimes been suspended; for in this case, we suppose, that an extraordinary cause has intervened. To believe, that a divine power has interposed to change the course of nature, is surely not the same thing, as to believe that the same cause which commonly produced one effect, is now attended by another entirely different. The natural causes, it is true, remain the same, but the general proposition slated above, is not true, if confined only to these. If there exist supernatural causes, or a power superior to the laws of nature,--and this our author does not profess to deny--then the laws of nature, or mere natural causes may remain the same; and yet, by the operation of these supernatural causes, effects entirely diverse from those that would be the sequence of natural causes, may take place, And the author himself seems in one place to, have been aware of this distinction, and to admonish the reader of its existence; and yet, through the

### The Evidences of the Christian Religion

whole of the argument he proceeds, as if the two propositions were identical. fie ought, however, to have recollected, that while no man in his senses disbelieves the first proposition, much the greater number of men have believed, that in some cases the laws of nature have been suspended; not, that they thought that the same causes did not, in these instances, produce the same effects, but that other causes of greater potency than natural causes, were put into operation.

When our author, therefore, infers from the uniformity of causation, that no testimony is sufficient to be the foundation of a rational belief, that there has been a deviation from the common course of nature, he applies a correct principle to a case to which it evidently does not belong. Because, the same cause must produce the same effects, does it follow, that when another and superior cause operates, the same effects must be produced? This would be in direct repugnance to his own maxim. Then, before this principle of the uniformity of causes and effects can he applied, it must be demonstrated, that in the case under consideration, no other causes operate, but such as are usual and natural, and whenever he shall be able to establish this, there will be no further contest respecting the matter.

That I do not misrepresent the argument of the author, wilt appear satisfactorily, by considering the cases which be has adduced. "Suppose, for instance," says he, "any person to affirm, that he had exposed a cubic Inch of ice to a temperature of 200 degrees of Fahrenheit, and that at the expiration of an hour, it had retained its solidity. Here is a sequence of events asserted, which is entirely at variance with the admitted course of nature; and the slightest reflection is sufficient to show, that to believe the assertion, would involve a logical absurdity, The intrinsic discrepancy of the facts could never be overcome by any possible proofs of the truth of testimony."

In another page, he says, "If a number of Men were to swear, that they had seen the mercury of the barometer remain at the height of thirty inches, when placed in the exhausted receiver of an air-pump, their testimony would be instantly rejected. The universal conclusion would be, that such an event was impossible." What is here so confidently asserted, would only be true upon the supposition, that no causes but such as were natural operated in the cases adduced; but on the hypothesis of the operation of a supernatural cause, there would be neither absurdity nor impossibility in either of the facts. What! could not He, who established these laws, and gave to heat and air, respectively, their peculiar powers and qualities, suspend their usual operation? Could not He, clause the ice to remain unmelted in any temperature; and the mercury to remain suspended, without the pressure of the atmosphere? But the sophistical nature of the argument used, is most evident. The principle is, that similar causes must have similar effects. Very good--what then? Why, if ice remain unmelted at 200 degrees of Fahrenheit, then this principle would be violated. I answer, not at all, provided another cause is in operation, of such potency as to counteract the usual effects of caloric; or to counteract the gravity of the quicksilver, in vacuo. And it will not do to allege, that God, who established these laws, will not contravene them, on any occasion; for this would be an entire change of the ground of the argument, and a relinquishment of the principle on which the reasoning of our author is founded. Besides, it would be a mere begging the question in dispute.

Now, in both the cases adduced by this writer, to illustrate and confirm his argument, on which he pronounces so confidently, that the judgment of men would universally reject any testimony, I beg leave to be of a different opinion, and will appeal to the common sense of all reflecting men, whether, on the supposition, that a dozen men of perspicacity and undoubted integrity, should solemnly affirm that they had seen a cubic inch of ice remain an hour unmelted at 200 degrees of Fahrenheit, whether they could refuse their assent? even if they knew of no good reason why the laws of nature should be suspended. But if they knew that an important purpose in the divine government could be answered by such a miracle, much less testimony would be sufficient to produce unwavering conviction of the truth of the extraordinary fact. And while they assent to such facts, on sufficient testimony; they are guilty of no absurdity, and violate no rule of common sense. It is true, that the credibility of the event reported, may be reduced to this question--whether is it more probable, that the laws of nature should, for a good end, be suspended, or that twelve men of tried veracity, should agree to assert a falsehood, without any motive to induce them to do so? And here our ingenious author revives the metaphysical balance or Mr. Hume; and after admitting that the evidence from testimony may be so strong that nothing is wanting to give it force, yet the maxim, that the same causes must have the same effects, is also a truth so certain, that no evidence can countervail it. We have, therefore, according to this statement, the equipoise of evidence, which we have already considered, in Mr. Hume's argument. The rational mina, in such circumstance, must remain neutral; it can neither believe nor disbelieve; for the evidence for the one exactly counterbalances that for the other. But after stating this hypothesis, our author finds that the evidence from testimony never can be so convincing, as that which we have for the uniformity of causation. His words are--"If the rejection and the admission of the testimony equally implied a deviation from the uniform sequence of causes and effects, there could be no reason for rejecting or admitting it."--"But the rejection of the testimony is not in this predicament. The causes of testimony, or in other words, those considerations which operate on the minds of the witness, cannot always be ascertained; and as we are uncertain as to the causes in operation, we cannot be certain of the effects, we cannot be sure that the circumstances of the witness are such as have given rise to true testimony, and consequently we cannot be sure that the testimony is true."

On this whole subject I have several remarks to make.--First, this method of destroying the equipoise of evidence granted by Mr. Hume, and conceded by himself, is not altogether fair; because it does not adroit what Is obviously true, that in regard to some kinds of testimony, the evidence is so certain, that we might as soon doubt of our own existence as of the truth of the facts attested. Now, this being the case, there was no propriety in representing all testimony as being involved in some degree of uncertainty.

Again, what is here said of testimony will apply just as fully to what we ourselves witness, and for the truth of which we have the testimony of our own senses. I mean, that if the argument of our author is at all valid, it will prove, that if we saw the ice remain unmelted in the heat, and beheld it ever so often; and found that thousands around us received the same impression, we must not credit our own senses, nor believe what we saw with our own eyes; because, however certain this kind of, evidence may be, it cannot be more certain, than the principle, that the same causes will uniformly produce the same effects. Therefore, although we should, under all manner of circumstances, see such events, they could not be believed; for to believe them would be a logical absurdity. And thus, would these men, by their metaphysics, reason us out of the evidence of our very eye-sight. I know, indeed, that neither Hume, nor the author whose reasoning, we are now considering, have pushed the argument to this its just consequence; but I would defy any man to show, that it is not as applicable to the evidence of the senses as to that derived from testimony. Now, as the kind of evidence which will invariably command assent, is not learned by metaphysical reasoning, but by experience, I would leave the matter to be decided by every man of impartial judgment, for himself. Every man knows, whether or not, he would believe his own eyes, if lie should see ice remain unmelted in 200 degrees of temperature, according to Fahrenheit: or would be say, it seems to be so, but it cannot be true, because it contradicts a self-evident principle, "that the same causes must always be followed by the same effects." To which a man of plain, unsophisticated common sense would reply, "I must believe my own senses; if doing so contradicts a thousand abstract principles, I care not--seeing is believing.'" And the same may be said in regard to testimony. Suppose a thousand persons entirely disinterested to aver, that they had seen ice remain unmelted in a very high temperature, we could not but believe them, account for the fact as we might. But we have already proved, that believing in such an event violates no maxim, but only supposes that some extraordinary power or cause is in operation; and when it is understood, that this deviation from the laws of nature is intended to confirm the declarations of some person who claims to be a messenger of God, there is not only no absurdity in the thing; but all presumption against the probability of such supernatural interposition is removed, as has been shown in the argument on that subject.

It might also be demonstrated, that upon the principles of this author, not only would it be absurd, upon any evidence, to believe in a fact which involved a real deviation from the laws of nature, but in any one which was entirely different from all our own experience of the laws of nature. For if it would be absurd to believe, on the testimony of thousands of unconnected witnesses that ice did not melt in a certain case when placed in the fire; then it was altogether rational for the king of Siam, and all others in similar circumstances, to disbelieve the fact, that water had been known to become as hard as a stone so that men and animals could walk upon it. Persons so situated never could know that. such an effect existed but by testimony; yet as this testimony contradicted all their own experience about the laws of nature, in relation to water, they ought rather to reject the testimony, however strong, than to credit a fact which seemed to involve a deviation from "the sequence of causes and effects," to use the language f this author. And thus we should be reduced to the necessity of rejecting all facts not consonant to our own personal experience; for to receive them on the ground of testimony, would be to violate the principle, that causation is uniform.

But the zeal of our author to establish his favorite point, has led him, not only to assert, that a deviation from the regular succession of the laws of nature was incredible, on the ground of testimony, but that it is, in the nature of things. impossible. In this assertion, he certainly may lay claim to originality; for I believe no one before him, not even Hume, has gone so far, in bold affirmation. His words are--"An event is impossible which contradicts our experience, or which implies that the same causes have produced different effects, or the same effects been preceded by different causes. Thus, when we pronounce that it was impossible for a piece of ice to remain in the midst of burning coals without being dissolved,. our conclusion involves a complete knowledge of this particular effect of fire on ice."

And he is so confident that this is the true import of the word impossible, that he says, "If I am not greatly deceived, the acutest reasoner, the closest thinker, the most subtle analyser of words, will find himself unable to produce any other meaning of the term, impossible, than that which is here assigned to it." But he seems to have felt that he had gone too far in this dogmatical, and I must say, irrational assertion; for in a note he gives himself, another, and one of the true meanings of the word, impossible. But as confident assertion, accompanied by no proof nor reason, is sufficiently answered by a confident

*The Evidences of the Christian Religion*

denial, I would take the liberty of saying, therefore, that if I am not greatly mistaken, no accurate philologist will admit, that this is the true meaning of the word, impossible. And certainly, men of plain common sense, never can be persuaded, that it is impossible for the succession of events according to the laws of nature, to be changed. It is true, when we confine our ideas to the mere powers and qualities of nature, we do assert that their effects will be uniform, and that it is impossible that the same causes should produce different effects; but when we extend our views to the Great FIRST CAUSE, it is not only absurd, but impious, to assert, that he cannot suspend or alter the laws of nature. Nothing is impossible to him which does not imply a contradiction, or is not repugnant to his attributes.

The conclusion which is rational on this subject, is, that all things are possible to God, and whatever is possible may be believed on sufficient testimony; which testimony, however, must be strong, in proportion to the improbability of the. event to be confirmed.

## NOTE B

Mohammed asserted, that while he was in his bed one night, the Angel Gabriel knocked at his door, and that when he went out, he saw him with seventy pair of expanded wings, whiter than snow, and clearer than chrystal. The angel informed him that he had come to conduct him to heaven; and directed him to mount an animal, which stood ready at the door, and which was between the nature of an ass and a mule. They name of this beast was Alborak, in color whiter than milk, and swift as lightning. But when the prophet went to mount, the animal proved refractory, and he could not seat himself upon its back, until he promised it a place in Paradise.

The journey from Mecca to Jerusalem was performed in the twinkling of an eye. When he arrived at the latter place, the departed prophets and saints came forth to meet him, and saluted him. Here, he found a ladder of light, and tying Alborak to a rock, he followed Gabriel on the ladder, until they arrived at the first heaven, where admittance was readily granted by the porter, when he was told by Gabriel, that the person who accompanied him, was Mohammed, the prophet of God. Here, he met an old decrepit man, who it seems was no other than our father Adam; and who greatly rejoiced at having so distinguished a son. He saw also innumerable angels, in the shape of birds, beasts, and men. This heaven was made of pure silver, and he saw the stars suspended from it, by chains of gold.

In like manner, he ascended to the second heaven, a distance of five hundred years journey, which was of pure gold, and contained twice as many angels as the former. Here, he met Noah. Thence he proceeded to the third, which was made of precious stones, where he met Abraham. The fourth was all of emerald, where he met Joseph, the son of Jacob. In the fifth, which was of adamant, lie met Moses. In the sixth, which was of carbuncle, he saw John the Baptist. In the seventh which was made of divine light, he saw Jesus Christ, and commended himself to his prayers. All the persons he had seen before, however, begged an interest in his prayers. Here Gabriel informed him, that he could go no further, and he proceeded alone, through snow and water, until he came near the throne of God, when he heard a voice, saying, "O Mohammed, salute thy Creator!" He was not permitted to come near the throne of the Almighty, on the right side of which he saw inscribed the sentence, there is no God but God, and Mohammed is his prophet; which is the fundamental article of the Mohammedan creed.

After being permitted to bold a long conversation with the Creator, he returned as he came, and found Alborak ready to convey him home, on whose back he swiftly glided again to Mecca. All this happened in the space of the tenth part of a night.

In the third heaven, he says, he saw an angel of so great a size, that the distance between his eyes, was of seventy thou. sand days journey. This was the angel of death, who has a large table before him on which he is ever writing and blotting out; whenever a name is blotted, the person immediately dies. He speaks also of another angel, in the sixth heaven; which had seventy thousand heads and as many tongues.

## NOTE C

The Abbe Paris was the oldest son of a counsellor of Paris, but being much inclined to a life of devotion, he relinquished his patrimony to his younger brother, and retired to an obscure part of Paris, where he spent his life in severe penance, and in charitable exertions, for the relief of the distressed poor, He was buried in the ground of the church of St. Medard, near the wall, where his brother erected a tomb-stone over the grave. To this spot many poor people, who knew his manner of life, came to perform their devotions, as much, probably out of feelings of gratitude, as any thing else. Some among the devotees who attended at this place, professed that they experienced a salutary change in their ailments. This being noised abroad, as the Abbe had been a jealous Jansenist, all who were of this party encouraged the idea of miracles having been performed; and multitudes who were indisposed, were induced to go to the tomb of the saint; and some, as they confessed before a competent tribunal, were persuaded to feign diseases which they never bad. It is a fact, however, that the greater part received no benefit, and that more diseases were produced than were cured; for, soon, many of the worshippers were seized with convulsions, from which procceeded the sect of Convulsionists, which attracted attention for many years. It was soon found expedient to close up the tomb; but cures were still said to be performed by the saint, on persons in distant places. The Jesuits exerted themselves to discredit the whole business, and the Archbishop of Paris had a judicial investigation made of a number of the most remarkable cases, the results of which were various, and often ludicrous. A young woman, said to have been cured at the tomb of blindness and lameness, was proved to have been neither blind nor lame. A man with diseased eyes was relieved, but it appeared that he was then using powerful medicine, and that after all, his eyes were not entirely healed. A certain Abbe who had the misfortune to have one of his legs shorter than the other, was persuaded that he experienced a sensible elongation of the defective limb, but on measurement no increase could be discovered. A woman in the same situation danced on the tomb daily, to obtain an elongation of a defective limb, and was persuaded that she received benefit; but it was ascertained, that she would have to dance there fifty-four years, before the cure would be effected, at the rate at which it was proceeding; but for the unfortunate Abbe, seventy-two years would have, been requisite. In short, the whole number of cures, after examination, was reduced to eight or nine, all of which can be easily accounted for, on natural principles; and in several of these instances, the cures were not perfect.

www.ingramcontent.com/pod-product-compliance
Lightning Source LLC
Chambersburg PA
CBHW032050090426
42744CB00004B/152